D0312555

AMERICAN POETS PROJECT

AMERICAN POETS PROJECT

IS PUBLISHED WITH A GIFT IN MEMORY OF

James Merrill

AND SUPPORT FROM ITS FOUNDING PATRONS

Sidney J. Weinberg, Jr. Foundation

The Berkley Foundation

Richard B. Fisher and Jeanne Donovan Fisher

Edith Wharton

selected poems

louis auchincloss editor

AMERICAN POETS PROJECT

THE LIBRARY OF AMERICA

Introduction, volume compilation, and notes copyright © 2005 by Literary Classics of the United States, Inc. All rights reserved. Printed in the United States of America. No part of this book may be reproduced in any manner whatsoever without permission.

Twelve Poems copyright © 1926. All uncollected and manuscript poems copyright © 2005 by the Estate of Edith Wharton and the Watkins Loomis Agency. Reprinted by permission.

The paper used in this publication meets the minimum requirements of the American National Standard for Information Sciences—Permanence of Paper for Printed Library Materials, ANSI Z39.48—1984.

Design by Chip Kidd and Mark Melnick.
Frontispiece: The Beinecke Rare Book and Manuscript Library, Yale University

Library of Congress Cataloging-in-Publication Data:
Wharton, Edith, 1862–1937.
  [Poems. Selections]
  Selected poems / Edith Wharton ; Louis Auchincloss, editor.
    p. cm. — (American poets project ; 18)
  Includes bibliographical references.
  ISBN 1–931082–86–3 (alk. paper)
  I. Auchincloss, Louis. II. Title. III. Series.

PS3545.H16A6 2005
811'.52— dc22

2005044163

10 9 8 7 6 5 4 3 2 1

Edith Wharton

CONTENTS

Artemis to Actæon, and Other Verse (1909)

INTRODUCTION

Edith Wharton's first poems appeared in a small, privately printed pamphlet, entitled *Verses*, when she was only sixteen. That her parents should have gone to the trouble and expense of producing this little collection goes far to rebut the statement so often made by her biographers that she grew up in an atmosphere of indifference to her creative talent. The poems are a remarkable achievement for a girl of that age—and some of them had been written as much as two years earlier. They show a fine if conventional appreciation of the beauties of nature, the transiency of first love, the power of memory over fleeting time, and the loveliness of fair women, but most of all they show the promise of their author. She had already mastered the knack of striking first lines such as: "I love the silver dawn of night / That melts the dark away," or "A cold grey sea, a cold grey sky / And leafless swaying boughs," or "We might have loved each other after all, / Have lived and learned together!"

Wharton's reputation has never depended on her poetry, which is only a minor portion of her works, and some critics have deemed it too coolly intellectual for the first rank. Though this could not be said of her posthumously discovered love poems, it should in any case not derogate from our high estimate of the fineness of much of her published verse. Wharton cannot be compared with Keats or Shelley, but she had an unfailing ear for the right word, the right tone. It can be said of her that she never wrote a bad book. It might almost be said that she never wrote a bad line.

"The Last Token," in *Verses*, inspired by an academic painting of a Christian girl in the Roman arena about to be devoured by big cats and clutching a flower tossed to her by her lover safely ensconced with the audience above, represents her first experiment with the Browningesque dramatic monologue that she was later to perfect. The lover might be a forecast of Lawrence Selden in *The House of Mirth*, the cultivated dilettante who can do little more for his ill-fated sweetheart than toss her a rose from his own high immunity.

Poetry was important to Wharton because it enabled her to express the deeply emotional side of her nature that she kept under such tight control, not only in her life but in the ordered sweep of her fiction. In *A Backward Glance* she describes vividly the explosive effect on a young girl of opening a volume of Swinburne and having this stanza "burst into fiery bloom" in her hands:

Forth, ballad, and take roses in both arms,
  Even till the top rose touch thee in the throat
Where the least thornprick harms;
  And girdled in thy golden singing-coat,
Come thou before my lady and say this:
  Borgia, thy gold hair's colour burns in me,
Thy mouth makes beat my blood in feverish rhymes;
  Therefore as many as these roses be,
    Kiss me so many times.

It was not until 1909, when she was 47, that Wharton published her next volume of poetry, *Artemis to Actæon*, though she had contributed verse to periodicals. Some of this collection seems almost surely to have been inspired by her only love affair of which we have any knowledge, her liaison, strictly secret as she was not yet divorced from Edward Wharton, with Morton Fullerton, which is believed to have lasted from 1908 to 1911.

In her preface to *Eternal Passion in English Poetry* (1939), an anthology that she compiled with Robert Norton, Wharton wrote that "the rank taken by love poems in the total production of each poet is almost always in inverse ratio to the greatness of the poet." If you substitute the word "writer" for "poet" at the end of the quotation, it is certainly true of Wharton herself. Love has to share the pages of her fiction with a multitude of other emotions. As R.W.B. Lewis has put it: "For her novels and stories Edith Wharton drew systematically on incidents, persons and places she had herself known; but for the expression of her most private and vital emotions she turned to poetry."

So much has been written of the affair with Fullerton, which ultimately dwindled for her into disillusionment and nostalgic friendship, that it is sometimes a bit difficult not to think of it in reading *Artemis to Actæon*. The picture of Wharton, the great lady of letters, doffing "her raiment by the Attic flood" and becoming a "wild woodland woman" (as in "The Mortal Lease") may arouse a vulgar snicker. But this should be resisted. We know, after all, however tritely, the kinship of the colonel's lady and Rosie O'Grady. It is always sad to see a first-class person in the grip of a third-class one, and Fullerton was certainly the latter, with his lies and affairs with both sexes and his inducing Wharton to pay off his blackmail threats. She once wrote that she would have been better off had she never met him, but he nonetheless gave her the deepest emotional experience of her lifetime, and she was always grateful for that. She never forgot that she had once addressed him as "my adored, my one love, you who have given me the only moments of real life I have ever known." And she always looked back bitterly on the subterfuges she had had to practice to keep the affair secret, confessing to one friend: "Ah, the poverty, the miserable poverty, of any love that lies outside of marriage, of any love that is not living together, a sharing of all!"

The eight sonnets that make up "The Mortal Lease" in *Artemis* are among her finest poems. They tell the story of the narrator's frustrated desire to give herself entirely to her lover and her subsequent desperate need to see all that she has not dared to achieve sublimated in a single kiss. The sonnets contrast the eternal with the finite, seeking to find the former in the latter, with which mortals have to be content. At first the speaker asks if love, even if it spring from the muddy origins of matter, be not in some way the fruit of man's immortal gains. With a kiss do we not wing "the vistas of infinity"? But no, she cannot turn herself into "the nymph who danced / Smooth by Ilissus as the plane-tree's bole" or the "Nereid whose drenched lashes glanced / Like sea-flowers through the summer sea's long roll"; she is held back by inhibitions, like the nun clasping her "Bridegroom in her soul." The lover responds by urging her to "live to-day," but she limits him to the kiss, trying to persuade herself that "in that moment . . . we live enough." Yet the ghost of that departed moment tells her that now she will never know the cup the gods have offered her. She insists, however, with a wonderful eloquence, that she will.

> Shall I not know? I, that could always catch
> The sunrise in one beam along the wall,
> The nests of June in April's mating call,

And ruinous autumn in the wind's first snatch
At summer's green impenetrable thatch—

"Vesalius in Zante," a dramatic monologue, strikes a plangent note of changing mood in the poems of *Artemis*. Now we hear the voice, no longer of the middle-aged woman who has become, however self-consciously, obsessed with the belated discovery of her own libido, but of the clear-minded, all-observing priestess of the life of reason, the great novelist of morals and manners, the author of *The House of Mirth* and *Ethan Frome*. "Vesalius" can stand up against almost any monologue of Browning's; only "My Last Duchess" is its superior.

It is cast in the form of the dying declaration of the famous 16th-century anatomist who was disciplined by the Church for dissecting, though in the interests of science, the body of a woman supposedly dead but actually still breathing. He later abandoned his research for a lofty but creatively idle position in the Spanish court. The eloquence of the old man's deep regret that he should have given up the noble and spiritually uplifting search for truth in his study of the human body is tense and moving, and his defense of cutting into the flesh of an almost expired woman is dramatically expressed. After all, mankind gained by what he did, and for the poor, presumably unconscious woman, about to die anyway, "her vain life ripened to this bud of death." What had Vesalius learned from his experiment?

For, just because her bosom fluttered still,
It told me more than many rifled graves.

Perhaps the most interesting part of the monologue is that where Vesalius sorrowfully compares his own aborted career with the triumphant one of his fellow Venetian, Ignatius Loyola, who represented his opposite in thought as one "resolved / To hold the wall of dogma against fact."

Ah, how I pitied him, mine own eyes set
Straight in the level beams of Truth, who groped
In error's old deserted catacombs
And lit his tapers upon empty graves!
Ay, but he held his own, the monk—more man
Than any laurelled cripple of the wars . . .

"Margaret of Cortona," also conceived as a dying dec-
laration, this one of the cloistered nun to whom the effigy
of Christ thrice bowed his head, is her death-bed confes-
sion that she would never have come to the convent had
the dear lover with whom she had rapturously lived in sin
not been killed by an enemy. "Think you I would not leave
this Christ for that?" she asks the scandalized priest who is
attending her last hour. But the head of Christ again bows
His forgiveness. Wharton in these verses seems to have
reconciled her own adulterous love with her faith. Not that
we know just what her faith was, but she had *Ave crux spes
unica* engraved on her tombstone. And yet she could
clearly contemplate, as in "An Autumn Sunset," the possi-
bility of a total extinction of the personality in "the melan-
choly unconsoling fold" of "all things that go utterly to
death."

Shall Time not ferry me to such a shore,
Over such sailless seas,
To walk with hope's slain importunities
In miserable marriage?

Could her use of the word "marriage" have been an
unconscious (or conscious) evocation of her own long trial
with her mentally decomposing spouse?

Twelve Poems, which Wharton published in 1926, is
largely made up of verses richly descriptive of the beauties
of nature: nightingales in Provence, "golden islands lapped

in gold," a roofless temple high in the hills, the mistral in the maquis. The poems evoke lovely pictures, certainly; they read aloud sonorously, but I find them a bit too elaborately ornamental, a touch too artificial. The "fane's august / Intercolumniations" and the "blue sea's unalterable calm / That ever like a slow-swung mirror rocks / The balanced breasts of sea birds" seem strained.

There is, however, a stirring poem, "With the Tide," an elegy on the death of Theodore Roosevelt, though his name is not mentioned, the date January 6, 1919, being deemed sufficient identification, which it perhaps was to contemporaries. She likens the deceased president to a dead man seated on a beach and hailed by an incoming vessel full of the faces of his dead friends. Except in the case of this "great American" he is welcomed by a whole flotilla of the ships that he has launched and manned. She ends the poem like Tennyson's "Ulysses" on a note of further noble adventure. The ships

> That now, returning from their sacred quest
> With the thrice-sacred burden of their dead,
> Lay waiting there to take you forth with them,
> Out on the flood-tide, to some farther quest.

"La folle du logis" is a beautiful paean to the spirit goddess of imagination and adventure who has acted as the guide and mentor of the poet during a long and variegated lifetime. "Yet farther have I fared with you," the poet ends her address to the spirit, "and known / Love and his sacred tremors,"

> And creeping down by waterless defiles
> Under an iron midnight, have I kept
> My vigil in the waste till dawn began
> To walk among the ruins, and I saw

A sapling rooted in a fissured plinth,
And a wren's nest in the thunder-threatening hand
Of some old god of granite. . . .

Besides her collected poetry Wharton wrote a considerable number of other poems, some published in newspapers and magazines and some discovered in manuscript after her death. During the war she wrote several fervent lyrics, for during all of its four years she was a passionate war worker and promoter of the Allied cause, but these verses, like so much of the literature engendered by the fury of armageddon, are largely of historic interest today. Of the other published poetry, little is of the quality of the verse in *Artemis*, except for "Ogrin the Hermit."

It is again a dramatic monologue, her happiest form, told by the old hermit who harbors the lovers Tristan and Iseult, who have fled from the jealous wrath of Iseult's husband, King Mark. Although disapproving of their guilty conduct, he nonetheless allows them to build and occupy a hut in the shadow of the cross that he hopes will keep them from further sinning at night. But when the beguiling Iseult talks to him about her love, he comes to see it not as a sin at all, but as something fine and beautiful which arouses the old benignant pagan gods long-hidden in the woods and which is of the essence of life itself. For all his religious inhibitions the poor anchorite recognizes that a great vision has swept his eyes "with the fringe of fire," and he goes to Tintagel to procure for Iseult the raiment appropriate for her to wear when she returns to her husband.

For meet it was that a great Queen should pass
Crowned and forgiven from the face of Love.

There is also a very fine sonnet, "Euryalus," in which Sicilians of ancient time are seen on a holiday climbing to the hilltop fort near Syracuse to see the wonderful summer view and are appalled to witness instead the invading navy of the Greeks.

> There, on the ruined rampart climbing high,
> We sat and dreamed among the browsing sheep,
> Until we heard the trumpet's startled cry
> Waking a clang of arms about the keep,
> And seaward saw, with rapt foreboding eye,
> The sails of Athens whiten on the deep.

Among the poems that Wharton never intended to publish, along with the secret diary in which she enshrined the story of her love affair with Fullerton, is "Terminus," a 52-line hexameter lyric reminiscent of the style of Longfellow, or even of Whitman. It describes, with total candor and graphic realism, highly unusual in either her verse or prose, the night of June 4, 1909, which she spent surreptitiously with her lover in a seedy railroad hotel, the Charing Cross. The setting and what occurred there were both new to Wharton. As her friend Mrs. Winthrop Chanler once put it, Edith's one drawback as a traveling companion was her extreme fussiness about the condition and service in hotels. The best was never good enough for her. Nor had her perhaps unconsummated marriage prepared her for anything like the excitement that Fullerton offered. A novel ecstasy was united with a novel disgust. Wharton, for once in her life, was living as the common multitude of women lived. And she was humble about it, grateful for it, and like all great writers, eager to put it in words. She may have penned this poem on the very morning after. We know she mailed it to Fullerton a few weeks later.

The "common-place room" with its "dull, impersonal furniture," so unfamiliar to the author of the elegant *Decoration of Houses*, nonetheless "kindled a mystic flame." The "low wide bed, as rutted and worn as a high-road," the bed "that has borne the weight of fagged bodies, dust-stained, averted in sleep" is the scene of the awakening of her heart. The poet identifies herself with the other women who have slept there:

> And lying there hushed in your arms, as the waves
>   of rapture receded,
> And far down the margin of being we heard the low
>   beat of the soul,
> I was glad as I thought of those others, the
>   nameless, the many,
> Who perhaps thus had lain and loved for an hour on
>   the brink of the world,
> Secret and fast in the heart of the whirlwind of
>   travel,
> The shaking and shrieking of trains, the night-long
>   shudder of traffic . . .

But the poem ends on a sombre note. The lover, like other free men, will go off to "the wide flare of cities, with windy garlands and shouting," while the married woman is doomed to "waste lands & stretches of low-skied marsh, / To a harbourless wind-bitten shore." Wharton herself was returning dutifully to her husband and resolved to pick up her old life. What she thought she might be drinking in the departing kiss that she implanted on the lips of her still sleeping lover was oblivion. She did not know then that she had ahead of her the pangs of disillusionment. Such is life, or at least such was hers. But she would always have the consolation of her art.

Louis Auchincloss
2005

Sonnets

I. Le Viol d'Amour
(An Organ-stop.)

O soft, caressing sound, more sweet than scent
Of violets in woody hollows! Tone
As amorous as the ring-dove's tender moan
Beneath the spreading forest's leafy tent;
What mystery of earth or air hath lent
Thee that bewitching music, where the drone
Of Summer bees in dewy buds new blown
With trembling, fainting melody is blent?
What master did conceive thee, as the sound
Most fit to woo his lady from her rest,
What wakeful maiden in thy wooing found
The passion of her lover first exprest,
And from her silken pillows, beauty-crowned,
Stept forth and smiled on him who loved her best?

November 10th, 1875.

II. Vespers

It is the vesper hour, and in yon aisle
Where fainting incense clouds the heavy air
My lady's kneeling at her evening prayer,
Alone and silently; for in a file

The choristers have passed, and left her there,
Where martyrs from the tinted windows stare,
And saints look downward with a holy smile
Upon her meek devotions, while the day
Fades slowly, and a tender amber light
From coloured panes about her head doth play—
Her veil falls like a shade, and ghostly white
Her clasped hands glimmer through the deepening gray;
So will she kneel, until from Heaven's height
The Angels bend to hear their sister pray.

November 11th, 1875.

III. Bettine to Goethe

"Be friendly, pray, with these fancies of mine."
BETTINE.

Could youth discrown thy head of its gray hair,
I could not love it as I love it now;
Could one grand line be smoothed from thy brow,
'Twould seem to me less stately and less fair.
O no, be as thou art! For thou dost wear
The signs of noble age that cannot bow
Thine intellect like thy form, and I who know
How each year that did visibly impair
Thy first fresh youth, left inwardly such grand
And gracious gifts, would rather have thee so—
Believe me, master, who erect doth stand
In soul and purpose, age cannot lay low,
Till he receive, new from the Father's hand,
The youth he did but outwardly forego.

April 1876.

Spring Song

"O primavera! Gioventù dell'anno."

The first warm buds that break their covers,
   The first young twigs that burst in green,
The first blade that the sun discovers,
   Starting the loosened earth between.

The pale soft sky, so clear and tender,
   With little clouds that break and fly;
The crocus, earliest pretender
   To the low breezes passing by;

The chirp and twitter of brown builders,
   A couple in a tree, at least;
The watchful wisdom of the elders
   For callow younglings in the nest;

The flush of branches with fair blossoms,
   The deepening of the faint green boughs,
As leaf by leaf the crown grows fuller
   That binds the young Spring's rosy brows;

New promise every day of sweetness,
   The next bright dawn is sure to bring;
Slow breaking into green completeness,
   Fresh rapture of the early Spring!

May, 1876

I found a wee leaf in the cleft
Where the half-melted ice had left
A sunny corner, moist and warm,
For it to bud, beyond all harm.
    The wet, brown sod,
Long horned with ice, had slowly grown
So soft, the tender seedling blown
By Autumn winds, in earliest Spring
Sent through the sun-warmed covering,
    Its little leaf to God.

I found it there, beneath a ledge,
The dawning Spring time's fairest pledge,
And to my mind it dimly brought
The sudden, joyous, leafy thought
    Of Summer-time.
I plucked it from the sheltered cleft
Which the more kindly ice had left.
Within my hand to drop and die,
But for its sweet suggestions, I
    Revive it in rhyme.

1876.

Song

O Love, where are the hours fled,
    The hours of our young delight?
Are they forever gone and dead,
    Or only vanished out of sight?

O can it be that we shall live
    To know once more the joys gone by,
To feel the old, deep love revive,
    And smile again before we die?

Could I but fancy it might be,
    Could I the past bring back again,
And for one moment, holding thee,
    Forget the present and its pain!

O Love, those hours are past away
    Beyond our longing and our sighs—
Perhaps the Angels, some bright day,
    Will give them back in Paradise!

August, 1876.

Heaven

Not over roof and spire doth Heaven lie,
Star-sentinelled from our humanity,
Beyond the humble reach of every day.
And only near us when we weep or pray;

But rather in the household and the street,
Where loudest is the noise of hurrying feet,
Where hearts beat thickest, where our duties call,
Where watchers sit, where tears in silence fall.
We know not, or forget, there is no line
That marks our human off from our divine;
For all one household, all one family
In different chambers labouring are we;
God leaves the doors between them open wide,
Knowing how life and death are close allied,
And though across the threshold, in the gloom,
We cannot see into that other room,
It may be that the dear ones watching there
Can hear our cry of passionate despair,
And wait unseen to lead us through the door
When twilight comes, and all our work is o'er.

January, 1877.

"Maiden, Arise"

She, whom through life her God forbade to hear
The voices of her nearest and most dear,
So that she dwelt, amid the hum and rush
Of cities, in a vast, eternal hush,
Yet heard the first low calling of the voice
That others had not heeded in the noise,
And rising, when it whispered "Come with me,"
Followed the form that others could not see,
Smiling, perchance, in death at last to hear

The voices of the Angels fill her ear,
While the great, silent void that closed her round
Was overflowed with rippled floods of sound,
And the dumb past in Alleluias drowned.

March, 1877.

Spring

A Fragment

HILDEGARD.
It is the time when everything
Is flusht with presage of the Spring,
With every leaf and twig and bud
Feels new life rushing like a flood
Through greening veins and bursting tips;
When every hour a sunbeam slips
Across a sleepy flower's mouth,
And wakes it, babbling of the South;
When birds are doubtful where or how
To hang their nests on trunk or bough,
And all that is in wood or croft
Beneath an influence balmy-soft
Towards the light begins to strive,
Feeling how good it is to live!

WALTHER.
How beautiful thou standest there,
Thyself a prophet of the May!

The shining of thy golden hair
    Would melt December's snows away,
The roses on thy cheeks would woo
    Forth envious blossoms from their sleeps,
And robins plume their breasts anew
    To mock the crimson of thy lips.

HILDEGARD.

But where would be the golden tresses,
With ribands bravely intertwined
And where the roses, that thy praises
Have opened like a Summer wind,
Wert thou, my love, my Knight, not here,
To make these empty beauties dear?
The Spring would never deck her train
In such a fair and winsome wise
Did she not seek by smiles to chain
The sun her royal lover's eyes.

1876.

May Marian

A Ballad

In our town there dwelt a maiden
    Whom the folk called Marian;
In her narrow gabled casement
    All day long she sat and span.

Till a gentleman came riding
   Through our town one Summer day,
Spied May Marian at the casement,
   Stole her silly heart away.

Then she up and left her spinning,
   Laid aside her russet gown,
In a footboy's cap and mantle
   Followed him to London town.

There he led her to a mansion
   Standing by the river side;
"In that mansion dwells the lady
   Who is my betrothed bride;

"Gif thou 'lt be her serving maiden,
   Thou shalt wear a braw red gown,
Follow her to mass on Sunday
   Through the streets of London town;

"But if thou 'lt not be her maiden,
   Turn about and get thee home;
'Tis not meet that country wenches
   Through the city here should roam."

Not a word in answer spake she;
   Weeping sore she turned away,
And alone she gat her homeward,
   Travelling till the fall of day.

To our town she came at gloaming,
  Softly tirled she at the door;
Whispered: "let me in, sweet mother,
  I will wander never more."

"I will turn me to spinning,
  I will don my russet gown;
Home is best for country lasses,
  Men are all false in London town."

But the door was shut against her,
  To her prayers no answer none.
All night long alone she wandered,
  Wandered weeping through our town.

But at dawn she was aweary—
  In the street she laid her down;
And they found her dead at sunrise
  With her head upon a stone.

    MORAL.
Ladies, listen to my ballad:
  Maidens are too lightly won;
Home is best for country lasses,
  Men are false in London town.

1876.

Opportunities

Who knows his opportunities? They come
Not trumpet-tongued from Heaven, but small and
    dumb,
Not beckoning from the future's promised land,
But in the narrow present close at hand.
They walk beside us with unsounding feet,
And like those two that trode the Eastern street
And with their Saviour bartered thought for thought,
Our eyes are holden and we know them not.

1878.

"The Last Token"

A.D. 107.

(She speaks.)
One minute more of life! Enough to snatch
This flower to my bosom, and to catch
The parting glance and signal overhead
From one who sits and waits to see me dead.
One minute more! Enough to let him see
How straight the message fell from him to me,
And how, his talisman upon my breast,
I'll face the end as calmly as the rest.—
Th' impassive wall of faces seems to break
And shew one face aquiver for my sake * * *
How different death seems, with a hand that throws
Across the pathway of my doom a rose,

How brief and paltry life, compared to this
O'ertoppling moment of supremest bliss! * * *
Farewell! I feel the lions' hungry breath,
I meet your eyes * * * beloved, this is death.

1878.

Raffaelle to the Fornarina

(*Sitting to him for a Madonna.*)

Knot up the filmy strands of golden hair
That veil your breast, yet leave its beauties bare;
In decent ripples backward let it flow,
Smooth-parted sideways from your placid brow.
Unclasp the clinging necklace from your throat,
And let this misty veil about you float,
As round the seraphs of my visions swim
Faint, roseate clouds to make their radiance dim
And bearable to dazzled human eyes,
Uplifted in a rapture of surprise.
Lay off your armlets now, and cover up
With dark blue folds that shoulder's dimpled slope;
Let naught appear to woo the grosser sense,
But ruling calm, and sacred innocence;
Subdue the pointed twinkle of your eye
Into a level, large serenity,
(Now comes the test) and let your mouth awhile
Be pressed into a faint, ascetic smile,
A pure reflection of the inward thought,
A chastened glow from fires celestial caught.

1878.

Chriemhild of Burgundy

A Fragment

In all the land was not a maid
Could match her beauty white and red;
No decent veil she need to wear,
Deep-mantled in her royal hair,
Dun ripples, shot all through and through
With fiery gold; her eyes were blue
And clearer than a Summer wave
That murmurs in some sunless cave,
And over them her brow shone white,
Like the first low star that pricks the night,
And under them her mouth did redden,
Like ripe red clover, honey-laden;
But white as pear-bloom was her chin,
An elvish dimple played therein;
Her breast stirred softly up and down
Beneath the folding of her gown
As if a bird were prisoned there
That fluttered for the outer air,
And round and comely was each limb,
As doth a royal maid beseem.

1878.

Some Woman to Some Man

We might have loved each other after all,
Have lived and learned together! Yet I doubt it;
You asked, I think, too great a sacrifice,

Or else, perhaps, I rate myself too dear.
Whichever way the difference lies between us,
Would common cares have helped to lessen it,
A common interest, and a common lot?
Who knows indeed? We choose our path, and then
Stand looking back and sighing at our choice,
And say: "Perhaps the other road had lead
To fruitful valleys dozing in the sun."
Perhaps—perhaps—but all things are perhaps,
And either way there lies a doubt, you know.
We've but one life to live, and fifty ways
To live it in, and little time to choose
The one in fifty that will suit us best,
And so the end is, that we part, and say:
"We might have loved each other after all!"

1878.

Lines on Chaucer

No human pomp suggests his name,
No human pride builds up his fame,
But croft and meadow every where
His presence and his charm declare.

He was an echo of the woods,
A breath of vernal solitudes,
An annalist of brooks and birds,
Interpreter of sylvan words;

He worshipt nature where he trod
And still, through nature, worshipt God;
And spotless as the flower he praises
His name still blossoms with the daisies.

What We Shall Say Fifty Years Hence, of Our Fancy-Dress Quadrille

(*Danced at Swanhurst, August 8th, 1878.*)

Do you remember, long ago,
   Our Fancy-dress Quadrille?
Though many a year is past since then
   It makes me joyous still,
To think what fun we used to have
   When we were young and gay
And danced upon the Swanhurst lawn,
   That happy Summer day.

As Shepherd and as Sheperdess
   We trod the graceful round,
In pinks and blues, with buckled shoes,
   And crooks with ribands bound;
And as with joyous step we danced
   We gaily sang in time
The foolish words and merry tune
   Of some old Nursery rhyme.

But often through the singing broke
   A burst of laughter gay,

So young were we, so glad and free,
    That happy Summer day!
And hand in hand would linger long,
    As through the dance we moved,
For some of us were lovers then,
    And some of us were loved.

Ah, many a year is past since then,
    And fled the merry throng,
And yet I hear, at times quite clear,
    The echo of our song;
And though our days are Wintry now
    I well remember still
The happy Summer day we danced
    Our fancy-dress Quadrille!

1878.

Nothing More

'T was the old, old story told again,
    The story we all have heard;
A glimpse of brightness, parting and pain—
    You know it word for word.

A stolen picture—a faded rose—
    An evening hushed and bright;
A whisper—perhaps a kiss—who knows?
    A handclasp, and "goodnight."

The sum of what we call "first love,"
    That dreamflower rare and white,
That puts its magic blossom forth
    And dies in a single night.

1878.

June and December

When our eyes grow dim and our hair turns grey
    And we sit by the fire together,
'T will seem strange to talk in a shivering way
    Of our Summertime's rosy weather;

When our eyes were bright, and our tresses smooth,
    And the blood in our veins leapt read,
In the golden dawn of our long lost youth,
    With the promise of life ahead.

Shall we talk with smiles or with signs that day
    Of the years that are dead and gone,
Of the cares and the joys that have passed away
    Like dewdrops beneath the sun?

Nay, perchance we 'll see but the sunny side
    Of the vision, in looking back,
And the trace of joys that are past may abide,
    Where our sorrows have left no track;

And perhaps both the joys and the cares may seem
    In the light of that later day,
Like the phantom shapes of some beautiful dream
    That has long ago passed away.

But whate'er beside we may lose or hold
    From the hoards of the golden past,
May the friends we loved in the days of old
    To our hearts and thoughts cling fast,

And before the days come that are coming soon,
    And whose motto is "I remember,"
God grant us one vision of love and June
    To brighten our life's December.

October 7th, 1878.

October

A cold grey sea, a cold grey sky
    And leafless swaying boughs.
A wind that wanders sadly by,
    And moans about the house.

And in my lonely heart a cry
    For days that went before;
For joys that fly, and hopes that die,
    And the past that comes no more.

A Woman I Know

For a look from her eyes, for a smile of her mouth
Any man might well give the best years of his youth;
For the touch of her hand, for the warmth of her kiss
Might well barter his chances of infinite bliss;

For her step is like sunlight that plays on the sea
And her bosom is snowy as snowy can be,
And her hair is a mantle inwoven with gold
Such as Queens might have worn in the legends of old;

And her chin oh so white, and her cheek oh so red,
They might well drive a man who should look at them
    mad;
But beneath the bright breast where her heart ought to be,
What is there? Why a trap to catch fools, sir, like me!

October, 1878.

Daisies

Daisies, does he love me?
    Daisies, tell me true.
"Loves me * * * does not love me" * * *
    That will never do!
Why, you know, you daisies,
    Whatever you may say,
He stole that knot of riband
    I wore the other day.

Daisies, one more trial;
    Let your petals fall.
"Loves me * * * does not love me * * *
    Loves me," after all!
Thank you, darling daisies,
    And if it ends that way
I'll wear you in a garland
    Upon my wedding day.

1878.

Impromptu

(*On being asked for some verses.*)

I love the silver dawn of night
    That melts the dark away;
The ecstacy of pallid light
    That bathes the ended day;

When leaf by leaf the slumbrous trees
    Begin to talk anew;
And that sweet almoner, the breeze,
    Fills every cup with dew;

When on the fevered brow of toil
    Eve lays a soothing palm,
And whispers softly to the soul:
    "This hour was made for calm."

Notre Dame des Fleurs

To F. S. W.

Rosy, and fair, and fragrant,
    Your vassals, the flowers, come,
Bearing a welcome to us
    From the heart of your sunlit home;
Delicate garlands, wreathing
    With brightness these dreary hours;
Red lips and white lips, breathing
    Of you, our Lady of Flowers!

Violets, blue as your eyes are
    And roses, as soft as your cheek,—
Daphne, sweet as your words are,
    Primroses pallid and meek;
Feathery, waving fern-plumes,
    And blossoms from Summer bowers,
Each one bearing a message
    From you, our Lady of Flowers!

Giver of brightness and beauty,
    And Queen of this fragrant throng,
How shall we thank you or praise you
    But feebly in this poor song?
We, whom you crown with blossoms,
    Whom richly your kindness dowers,
We must be silent and love you,—
    Love you, our Lady of Flowers!

November 25, 1878.

Translations from the German

Three Songs from the German of Emanuel Geibel

I. ("Mein Pferd geht langsam durch die nacht.")

My steed goes slowly through the night;
    The moon is half in shadow,
With clouds that steal across her light
    Like lambs across a meadow.

A sudden stillness fills my heart,
    With grief so lately moved,
For in thy thoughts I have a part,
    Tonight, my best beloved.

In every whisper of the wind
    Thy greeting I discover;
O may'st thou in the breezes find
    The kisses of thy lover.

II. ("Schöne Lilie.")

Spotless lily in the garden,
    Fair and high on slender stem,
In the morning breeze thou wavest
    Like a dainty silver flame.

How thy chalice opens upward
    To admit the sunlight's gleam!
Scarce unto the earth belonging,
    Part of Heaven dost though seem.

Ah, thou bearest greetings to me
    From a being pure as thou,
Whom I called my spirit's spirit,
    Once with many a loving vow;

She who taught me to discover
    Love that lurks in sorrow's smart;
Now, if I but think upon her
    Sudden stillness fills my heart.

III.

There stands the ancient gabled house;
The rooms therein how well I know!
They're still as once they were, when first
        I loved there, long ago.

But, like the moon, times change, and hearts,
And strangers now the dwelling claim;
Another passion fills my breast;
        Yet is the house the same.

Today I went there to the feast;
Some memory made my bosom stir,
I heeded not the song and jest,
        I only thought of *her*,—

Of all that we had meant to be,
Of all my vanisht youthful years,
And of the love that filled her eyes,—
        Till mine o'erflowed with tears.

And when I roused me from the thought,
Alas, how changed did all things seem!
As though that dream had been my life,
    And all my life a dream.

Longing

From the German of Schiller

("Ach, aus dieses Thales Grùnden.")

From the shadows of the valley
  With the chilly mist opprest,
Might I only find the outlet
  I should count myself as blest.
There uprise the sunny mountains
  Green and young and fair to see,
Had I wings to lift me upward,
  To the mountains I would flee.

Melodies are sweetly chiming,
  I can catch the heavenly notes,
And a balmy flower fragrance
  On the light breeze downward floats.
Golden fruits are shining, glowing,
  Through the leafage, darkly green,
And the flowers that there are blowing
  Winter's snows have never seen.

Ah, how blissful must the life be
    In that sunshine without night;
Ah, how soft and how refreshing
    Is the air that crowns that height!
Yet the stormy river stays me
    That between us roars of death;
And its ghastly waves are lifted
    Till my spirit shuddereth.

There a bark all lonely tosses
    Without steersman, on the tide;
Leap into it, bold, untrembling,
    Sure some fate its sails will guide!
Thou must trust, and thou must venture,
    For the gods will lend no hand;
Nothing but a wonder lifts thee
    To thy golden Wonderland.

A Song

Freely Translated from the German of Ruckert

("Wie die Sonne sinkt am Abend.")

As at eve the sunlight dying
Wrapt in radiance sinks from sight,
As the Spring, the Autumn flying,
Still seems fragrant in her flight;
As our childhood's shining spirit
In Time's chariot whirls away;
As with unfulfilled wishes

Life steals past us day by day;
Thus thou fleddest, radiant darling
Of the Springtime's sunny breath,
And Hafiz alone encounters
Twilight, Autumn, Age and Death.

ARTEMIS TO ACTÆON, AND OTHER VERSE | 1909

I

Artemis to Actœon

Thou couldst not look on me and live: so runs
The mortal legend—thou that couldst not live
Nor look on me (so the divine decree)!
That saw'st me in the cloud, the wave, the bough,
The clod commoved with April, and the shapes
Lurking 'twixt lid and eye-ball in the dark.
Mocked I thee not in every guise of life,
Hid in girls' eyes, a naiad in her well,
Wooed through their laughter, and like echo fled,
Luring thee down the primal silences
Where the heart hushes and the flesh is dumb?
Nay, was not I the tide that drew thee out
Relentlessly from the detaining shore,
Forth from the home-lights and the hailing voices,
Forth from the last faint headland's failing line,
Till I enveloped thee from verge to verge
And hid thee in the hollow of my being?
And still, because between us hung the veil,
The myriad-tinted veil of sense, thy feet
Refused their rest, thy hands the gifts of life,
Thy heart its losses, lest some lesser face
Should blur mine image in thine upturned soul

Ere death had stamped it there. This was thy thought.
And mine?

    The gods, they say, have all: not so!
This have they—flocks on every hill, the blue
Spirals of incense and the amber drip
Of lucid honey-comb on sylvan shrines,
First-chosen weanlings, doves immaculate,
Twin-cooing in the osier-plaited cage,
And ivy-garlands glaucous with the dew:
Man's wealth, man's servitude, but not himself!
And so they pale, for lack of warmth they wane,
Freeze to the marble of their images,
And, pinnacled on man's subserviency,
Through the thick sacrificial haze discern
Unheeding lives and loves, as some cold peak
Through icy mists may enviously descry
Warm vales unzoned to the all-fruitful sun.
So they along an immortality
Of endless-vistaed homage strain their gaze,
If haply some rash votary, empty-urned,
But light of foot, with all-adventuring hand,
Break rank, fling past the people and the priest,
Up the last step, on to the inmost shrine,
And there, the sacred curtain in his clutch,
Drop dead of seeing—while the others prayed!
Yea, this we wait for, this renews us, this
Incarnates us, pale people of your dreams,
Who are but what you make us, wood or stone,
Or cold chryselephantine hung with gems,
Or else the beating purpose of your life,
Your sword, your clay, the note your pipe pursues,

The face that haunts your pillow, or the light
Scarce visible over leagues of labouring sea!
O thus through use to reign again, to drink
The cup of peradventure to the lees,
For one dear instant disimmortalised
In giving immortality!
So dream the gods upon their listless thrones.
Yet sometimes, when the votary appears,
With death-affronting forehead and glad eyes,
Too young, they rather muse, *too frail thou art,*
And shall we rob some girl of saffron veil
And nuptial garland for so slight a thing?
And so to their incurious loves return.

Not so with thee; for some indeed there are
Who would behold the truth and then return
To pine among the semblances—but I
Divined in thee the questing foot that never
Revisits the cold hearth of yesterday
Or calls achievement home. I from afar
Beheld thee fashioned for one hour's high use,
Nor meant to slake oblivion drop by drop.
Long, long hadst thou inhabited my dreams,
Surprising me as harts surprise a pool,
Stealing to drink at midnight; I divined
Thee rash to reach the heart of life, and lie
Bosom to bosom in occasion's arms,
And said: *Because I love thee thou shall die!*

For immortality is not to range
Unlimited through vast Olympian days,

Or sit in dull dominion over time;
But this—to drink fate's utmost at a draught,
Nor feel the wine grow stale upon the lip,
To scale the summit of some soaring moment,
Nor know the dulness of the long descent,
To snatch the crown of life and seal it up
Secure forever in the vaults of death!

And this was thine: to lose thyself in me,
Relive in my renewal, and become
The light of other lives, a quenchless torch
Passed on from hand to hand, till men are dust
And the last garland withers from my shrine.

Life

Nay, lift me to thy lips, Life, and once more
Pour the wild music through me—

   I quivered in the reed-bed with my kind,
Rooted in Lethe-bank, when at the dawn
There came a groping shape of mystery
Moving among us, that with random stroke
Severed, and rapt me from my silent tribe,
Pierced, fashioned, lipped me, sounding for a voice,
Laughing on Lethe-bank—and in my throat
I felt the wing-beat of the fledgeling notes,
The bubble of godlike laughter in my throat.

Such little songs she sang,
Pursing her lips to fit the tiny pipe,
They trickled from me like a slender spring
That strings frail wood-growths on its crystal thread,
Nor dreams of glassing cities, bearing ships.
She sang, and bore me through the April world
Matching the birds, doubling the insect-hum
In the meadows, under the low-moving airs,
And breathings of the scarce-articulate air
When it makes mouths of grasses—but when the sky
Burst into storm, and took great trees for pipes,
She thrust me in her breast, and warm beneath
Her cloudy vesture, on her terrible heart,
I shook, and heard the battle.

                              But more oft,
Those early days, we moved in charmèd woods,
Where once, at dusk, she piped against a faun,
And one warm dawn a tree became a nymph
Listening; and trembled; and Life laughed and passed.
And once we came to a great stream that bore
The stars upon its bosom like a sea,
And ships like stars; so to the sea we came.
And there she raised me to her lips, and sent
One swift pang through me; then refrained her hand,
And whispered: "Hear—" and into my frail flanks,
Into my bursting veins, the whole sea poured
Its spaces and its thunder; and I feared.

We came to cities, and Life piped on me
Low calls to dreaming girls,
In counting-house windows, through the chink of gold,
Flung cries that fired the captive brain of youth,
And made the heavy merchant at his desk
Curse us for a cracked hurdy-gurdy; Life
Mimicked the hurdy-gurdy, and we passed.

We climbed the slopes of solitude, and there
Life met a god, who challenged her and said:
"Thy pipe against my lyre!" But "Wait!" she laughed,
And in my live flank dug a finger-hole,
And wrung new music from it. Ah, the pain!

We climbed and climbed, and left the god behind.
We saw the earth spread vaster than the sea,
With infinite surge of mountains surfed with snow,
And a silence that was louder than the deep;
But on the utmost pinnacle Life again
Hid me, and I heard the terror in her hair.

Safe in new vales, I ached for the old pang,
And clamoured "Play me against a god again!"
"Poor Marsyas-mortal—he shall bleed thee yet,"
She breathed and kissed me, stilling the dim need.
But evermore it woke, and stabbed my flank
With yearnings for new music and new pain.
"Another note against another god!"
I clamoured; and she answered: "Bide my time.
Of every heart-wound I will make a stop,

And drink thy life in music, pang by pang.
But first thou must yield the notes I stored in thee
At dawn beside the river. Take my lips."

She kissed me like a lover, but I wept,
Remembering that high song against the god,
And the old songs slept in me, and I was dumb.

We came to cavernous foul places, blind
With harpy-wings, and sulphurous with the glare
Of sinful furnaces—where hunger toiled,
And pleasure gathered in a starveling prey,
And death fed delicately on young bones.

"Now sing!" cried Life, and set her lips to me.
"Here are gods also. Wilt thou pipe for Dis?"
My cry was drowned beneath the furnace roar,
Choked by the sulphur-fumes; and beast-lipped gods
Laughed down on me, and mouthed the flutes of hell.

"Now sing!" said Life, reissuing to the stars;
And wrung a new note from my wounded side.

So came we to clear spaces, and the sea.
And now I felt its volume in my heart,
And my heart waxed with it, and Life played on me
The song of the Infinite. "Now the stars," she said.

Then from the utmost pinnacle again
She poured me on the wild sidereal stream,
And I grew with her great breathings, till we swept

The interstellar spaces like new worlds
Loosed from the fiery ruin of a star.

Cold, cold we rested on black peaks again,
Under black skies, under a groping wind;
And Life, grown old, hugged me to a numb breast,
Pressing numb lips against me. Suddenly
A blade of silver severed the black peaks
From the black sky, and earth was born again,
Breathing and various, under a god's feet.
A god! A god! I felt the heart of Life
Leap under me, and my cold flanks shook again.
He bore no lyre, he rang no challenge out,
But Life warmed to him, warming me with her,
And as he neared I felt beneath her hands
The stab of a new wound that sucked my soul
Forth in a new song from my throbbing throat.

"His name—his name?" I whispered, but she shed
The music faster, and I grew with it,
Became a part of it, while Life and I
Clung lip to lip, and I from her wrung song
As she from me, one song, one ecstasy,
In indistinguishable union blent,
Till she became the flute and I the player.
And lo! the song I played on her was more
Than any she had drawn from me; it held
The stars, the peaks, the cities, and the sea,
The faun's catch, the nymph's tremor, and the heart
Of dreaming girls, of toilers at the desk,
Apollo's challenge on the sunrise slope,

And the hiss of the night-gods mouthing flutes of hell—
All, to the dawn-wind's whisper in the reeds,
When Life first came, a shape of mystery,
Moving among us, and with random stroke
Severed, and rapt me from my silent tribe.
All this I wrung from her in that deep hour,
While Love stood murmuring: "Play the god, poor
    grass!"

Now, by that hour, I am a mate to thee
Forever, Life, however spent and clogged,
And tossed back useless to my native mud!
Yea, groping for new reeds to fashion thee
New instruments of anguish and delight,
Thy hand shall leap to me, thy broken reed,
Thine ear remember me, thy bosom thrill
With the old subjection, then when Love and I
Held thee, and fashioned thee, and made thee dance
Like a slave-girl to her pipers—yea, thou yet
Shalt hear my call, and dropping all thy toys
Thou'lt lift me to thy lips, Life, and once more
Pour the wild music through me—

Vesalius in Zante

(*1564*)

Set wide the window. Let me drink the day.
I loved light ever, light in eye and brain—
No tapers mirrored in long palace floors,

Nor dedicated depths of silent aisles,
But just the common dusty wind-blown day
That roofs earth's millions.

                    O, too long I walked
In that thrice-sifted air that princes breathe,
Nor felt the heaven-wide jostling of the winds
And all the ancient outlawry of earth!
Now let me breathe and see.

                    This pilgrimage
They call a penance—let them call it that!
I set my face to the East to shrive my soul
Of mortal sin? So be it. If my blade
Once questioned living flesh, if once I tore
The pages of the Book in opening it,
See what the torn page yielded ere the light
Had paled its buried characters—and judge!

The girl they brought me, pinioned hand and foot
In catalepsy—say I should have known
That trance had not yet darkened into death,
And held my scalpel. Well, suppose I *knew*?
Sum up the facts—her life against her death.
Her life? The scum upon the pools of pleasure
Breeds such by thousands. And her death? Perchance
The obolus to appease the ferrying Shade,
And waft her into immortality.
Think what she purchased with that one heart-flutter
That whispered its deep secret to my blade!
For, just because her bosom fluttered still,
It told me more than many rifled graves;
Because I spoke too soon, she answered me,

Her vain life ripened to this bud of death
As the whole plant is forced into one flower,
All her blank past a scroll on which God wrote
His word of healing—so that the poor flesh,
Which spread death living, died to purchase life!

Ah, no! The sin I sinned was mine, not theirs.
Not *that* they sent me forth to wash away—
None of their tariffed frailties, but a deed
So far beyond their grasp of good or ill
That, set to weigh it in the Church's balance,
Scarce would they know which scale to cast it in.
But I, I know. I sinned against my will,
Myself, my soul—the God within the breast:
Can any penance wash such sacrilege?

When I was young in Venice, years ago,
I walked the hospice with a Spanish monk,
A solitary cloistered in high thoughts,
The great Loyola, whom I reckoned then
A mere refurbisher of faded creeds,
Expert to edge anew the arms of faith,
As who should say, a Galenist, resolved
To hold the walls of dogma against fact,
Experience, insight, his own self, if need be!
Ah, how I pitied him, mine own eyes set
Straight in the level beams of Truth, who groped
In error's old deserted catacombs
And lit his tapers upon empty graves!
Ay, but he held his own, the monk—more man
Than any laurelled cripple of the wars,

Charles's spent shafts; for what he willed he willed,
As those do that forerun the wheels of fate,
Not take their dust—that force the virgin hours,
Hew life into the likeness of themselves
And wrest the stars from their concurrences.

So firm his mould; but mine the ductile soul
That wears the livery of circumstance
And hangs obsequious on its suzerain's eye.
For who rules now? The twilight-flitting monk,
Or I, that took the morning like an Alp?
He held his own, I let mine slip from me,
The birthright that no sovereign can restore;
And so ironic Time beholds us now
Master and slave—he lord of half the earth,
I ousted from my narrow heritage.

For there's the sting! My kingdom knows me not.
Reach me that folio—my usurper's title!
Fallopius reigning, *vice*—nay, not so:
Successor, not usurper. I am dead.
My throne stood empty; he was heir to it.
Ay, but who hewed his kingdom from the waste,
Cleared, inch by inch, the acres for his sowing,
Won back for man that ancient fief o' the Church,
His body? Who flung Galen from his seat,
And founded the great dynasty of truth
In error's central kingdom?

                              Ask men that,
And see their answer: just a wondering stare
To learn things were not always as they are—

The very fight forgotten with the fighter;
Already grows the moss upon my grave!
Ay, and so meet—hold fast to that, Vesalius.
They only, who re-conquer day by day
The inch of ground they camped on over-night,
Have right of foothold on this crowded earth.
I left mine own; he seized it; with it went
My name, my fame, my very self, it seems,
Till I am but the symbol of a man,
The sign-board creaking o'er an empty inn.
He names me—true! *"Oh, give the door its due
I entered by. Only, I pray you, note,
Had door been none, a shoulder-thrust of mine
Had breached the crazy wall"*—he seems to say.
So meet—and yet a word of thanks, of praise,
Of recognition that the clue was found,
Seized, followed, clung to, by some hand now dust—
Had this obscured his quartering of my shield?

How the one weakness stirs again! I thought
I had done with that old thirst for gratitude
That lured me to the desert years ago.
I did my work—and was not that enough?
No; but because the idlers sneered and shrugged,
The envious whispered, the traducers lied,
And friendship doubted where it should have cheered
I flung aside the unfinished task, sought praise
Outside my soul's esteem, and learned too late
That victory, like God's kingdom, is within.
(Nay, let the folio rest upon my knee.
I do not feel its weight.) Ingratitude?

The hurrying traveller does not ask the name
Of him who points him on his way; and this
Fallopius sits in the mid-heart of me,
Because he keeps his eye upon the goal,
Cuts a straight furrow to the end in view,
Cares not who oped the fountain by the way,
But drinks to draw fresh courage for his journey.
That was the lesson that Ignatius taught—
The one I might have learned from him, but would
    not—
That we are but stray atoms on the wind,
A dancing transiency of summer eves,
Till we become one with our purpose, merged
In that vast effort of the race which makes
Mortality immortal.
                "He that loseth
His life shall find it": so the Scripture runs.
But I so hugged the fleeting self in me,
So loved the lovely perishable hours,
So kissed myself to death upon their lips,
That on one pyre we perished in the end—
A grimmer bonfire than the Church e'er lit!
Yet all was well—or seemed so—till I heard
That younger voice, an echo of my own,
And, like a wanderer turning to his home,
Who finds another on the hearth, and learns,
Half-dazed, that other is his actual self
In name and claim, as the whole parish swears,
So strangely, suddenly, stood dispossessed
Of that same self I had sold all to keep,
A baffled ghost that none would see or hear!

"Vesalius? Who's Vesalius? This Fallopius
It is who dragged the Galen-idol down,
Who rent the veil of flesh and forced a way
Into the secret fortalice of life"—
Yet it was I that bore the brunt of it!

Well, better so! Better awake and live
My last brief moment as the man I was,
Than lapse from life's long lethargy to death
Without one conscious interval. At least
I repossess my past, am once again
No courtier med'cining the whims of kings
In muffled palace-chambers, but the free
Friendless Vesalius, with his back to the wall
And all the world against him. O, for that
Best gift of all, Fallopius, take my thanks—
That, and much more. At first, when Padua wrote:
"Master, Fallopius dead, resume again
The chair even he could not completely fill,
And see what usury age shall take of youth
In honours forfeited"—why, just at first,
I was quite simply credulously glad
To think the old life stood ajar for me,
Like a fond woman's unforgetting heart.
But now that death waylays me—now I know
This isle is the circumference of my days,
And I shall die here in a little while—
So also best, Fallopius!
                    For I see
The gods may give anew, but not restore;
And though I think that, in my chair again,

I might have argued my supplanters wrong
In this or that—this Cesalpinus, say,
With all his hot-foot blundering in the dark,
Fabricius, with his over-cautious clutch
On Galen (systole and diastole
Of Truth's mysterious heart!)—yet, other ways,
It may be that this dying serves the cause.
For Truth stays not to build her monument
For this or that co-operating hand,
But props it with her servants' failures—nay,
Cements its courses with their blood and brains,
A living substance that shall clinch her walls
Against the assaults of time. Already, see,
Her scaffold rises on my hidden toil,
I but the accepted premiss whence must spring
The airy structure of her argument;
Nor could the bricks it rests on serve to build
The crowning finials. I abide her law:
A different substance for a different end—
Content to know I hold the building up;
Though men, agape at dome and pinnacles,
Guess not, the whole must crumble like a dream
But for that buried labour underneath.
Yet, Padua, I had still my word to say!
Let others say it!—Ah, but will they guess
Just the one word—? Nay, Truth is many-tongued.
What one man failed to speak, another finds
Another word for. May not all converge
In some vast utterance, of which you and I,
Fallopius, were but halting syllables?

So knowledge come, no matter how it comes!
No matter whence the light falls, so it fall!
Truth's way, not mine—that I, whose service failed
In action, yet may make amends in praise.
Fabricius, Cesalpinus, say your word,
Not yours, or mine, but Truth's as you receive it!
You miss a point I saw? See others, then!
Misread my meaning? Yet expound your own!
Obscure one space I cleared? The sky is wide,
And you may yet uncover other stars.
For thus I read the meaning of this end:
There are two ways of spreading light; to be
The candle or the mirror that reflects it.
I let my wick burn out—there yet remains
To spread an answering surface to the flame
That others kindle.

                Turn me in my bed.
The window darkens as the hours swing round;
But yonder, look, the other casement glows!
Let me face westward as my sun goes down.

Margaret of Cortona

Fra Paolo, since they say the end is near,
And you of all men have the gentlest eyes,
Most like our father Francis; since you know
How I have toiled and prayed and scourged and striven,

Mothered the orphan, waked beside the sick,
Gone empty that mine enemy might eat,
Given bread for stones in famine years, and channelled
With vigilant knees the pavement of this cell,
Till I constrained the Christ upon the wall
To bend His thorn-crowned Head in mute
    forgiveness . . .
Three times He bowed it . . . (but the whole stands
    writ,
Sealed with the Bishop's signet, as you know),
Once for each person of the Blessed Three——
A miracle that the whole town attests,
The very babes thrust forward for my blessing,
And either parish plotting for my bones——
Since this you know: sit near and bear with me.

I have lain here, these many empty days
I thought to pack with Credos and Hail Marys
So close that not a fear should force the door——
But still, between the blessed syllables
That taper up like blazing angel heads,
Praise over praise, to the Unutterable,
Strange questions clutch me, thrusting fiery arms,
As though, athwart the close-meshed litanies,
My dead should pluck at me from hell, with eyes
Alive in their obliterated faces! . . .
I have tried the saints' names and our blessed Mother's
Fra Paolo, I have tried them o'er and o'er,
And like a blade bent backward at first thrust
They yield and fail me——and the questions stay.
And so I thought, into some human heart,

Pure, and yet foot-worn with the tread of sin,
If only I might creep for sanctuary,
It might be that those eyes would let me rest . . .

Fra Paolo, listen. How should I forget
The day I saw him first? (You know the one.)
I had been laughing in the market-place
With others like me, I the youngest there,
Jostling about a pack of mountebanks
Like flies on carrion (I the youngest there!),
Till darkness fell; and while the other girls
Turned this way, that way, as perdition beckoned,
I, wondering what the night would bring, half hoping:
If not, this once, a child's sleep in my garret,
At least enough to buy that two-pronged coral
The others covet 'gainst the evil eye,
Since, after all, one sees that I'm the youngest——
So, muttering my litany to hell
(The only prayer I knew that was not Latin),
Felt on my arm a touch as kind as yours,
And heard a voice as kind as yours say "Come."
I turned and went; and from that day I never
Looked on the face of any other man.
So much is known; so much effaced; the sin
Cast like a plague-struck body to the sea,
Deep, deep into the unfathomable pardon——
(The Head bowed thrice, as the whole town attests).
What more, then? To what purpose? Bear with me!——

It seems that he, a stranger in the place,
First noted me that afternoon and wondered:

How grew so white a bud in such black slime,
And why not mine the hand to pluck it out?
Why, so Christ deals with souls, you cry——what then?
Not so! Not so! When Christ, the heavenly gardener,
Plucks flowers for Paradise (do I not know?),
He snaps the stem above the root, and presses
The ransomed soul between two convent walls,
A lifeless blossom in the Book of Life.
But when my lover gathered me, he lifted
Stem, root and all—ay, and the clinging mud—
And set me on his sill to spread and bloom
After the common way, take sun and rain,
And make a patch of brightness for the street,
Though raised above rough fingers——so you make
A weed a flower, and others, passing, think:
"Next ditch I cross, I'll lift a root from it,
And dress my window" . . . and the blessing spreads.
Well, so I grew, with every root and tendril
Grappling the secret anchorage of his love,
And so we loved each other till he died. . . .

Ah, that black night he left me, that dead dawn
I found him lying in the woods, alive
To gasp my name out and his life-blood with it,
As though the murderer's knife had probed for me
In his hacked breast and found me in each wound . . .
Well, it was there Christ came to me, you know,
And led me home——just as that other led me.
(*Just as that other?* Father, bear with me!)
My lover's death, they tell me, saved my soul,
And I have lived to be a light to men,

46

And gather sinners to the knees of grace.
All this, you say, the Bishop's signet covers.
But stay! Suppose my lover had not died?
(At last my question! Father, help me face it.)
I say: Suppose my lover had not died—
Think you I ever would have left him living,
Even to be Christ's blessed Margaret?
——We lived in sin? Why, to the sin I died to
That other was as Paradise, when God
Walks there at eventide, the air pure gold,
And angels treading all the grass to flowers!
He was my Christ——he led me out of hell——
He died to save me (so your casuists say!)——
Could Christ do more? Your Christ out-pity mine?
Why, *yours* but let the sinner bathe His feet;
Mine raised her to the level of his heart . . .
And then Christ's way is saving, as man's way
Is squandering——and the devil take the shards!
But this man kept for sacramental use
The cup that once had slaked a passing thirst;
This man declared: "The same clay serves to model
A devil or a saint; the scribe may stain
The same fair parchment with obscenities,
Or gild with benedictions; nay," he cried,
"Because a satyr feasted in this wood,
And fouled the grasses with carousing foot,
Shall not a hermit build his chapel here
And cleanse the echoes with his litanies?
The sodden grasses spring again——why not
The trampled soul? Is man less merciful
Than nature, good more fugitive than grass?"

And so——if, after all, he had not died,
And suddenly that door should know his hand,
And with that voice as kind as yours he said:
"Come, Margaret, forth into the sun again,
Back to the life we fashioned with our hands
Out of old sins and follies, fragments scorned
Of more ambitious builders, yet by Love,
The patient architect, so shaped and fitted
That not a crevice let the winter in——"
Think you my bones would not arise and walk,
This bruisèd body (as once the bruisèd soul)
Turn from the wonders of the seventh heaven
As from the antics of the market-place?
If this could be (as I so oft have dreamed),
I, who have known both loves, divine and human,
Think you I would not leave this Christ for that?

——I rave, you say? You start from me, Fra Paolo?
Go, then; your going leaves me not alone.
I marvel, rather, that I feared the question,
Since, now I name it, it draws near to me
With such dear reassurance in its eyes,
And takes your place beside me . . .
                                    Nay, I tell you,
Fra Paolo, I have cried on all the saints——
If this be devil's prompting, let them drown it
In Alleluias! Yet not one replies.
And, for the Christ there—is He silent too?
Your Christ? Poor father; you that have but one,
And that one silent——how I pity you!
He will not answer? Will not help you cast

The devil out? But hangs there on the wall,
Blind wood and bone——?
                           How if *I* call on Him——
I, whom He talks with, as the town attests?
If ever prayer hath ravished me so high
That its wings failed and dropped me in Thy breast,
Christ, I adjure Thee! By that naked hour
Of innermost commixture, when my soul
Contained Thee as the paten holds the host,
Judge Thou alone between this priest and me;
Nay, rather, Lord, between my past and present,
Thy Margaret and that other's—whose she is
By right of salvage—and whose call should follow!
Thine? Silent still. ——— Or his, who stooped to her,
And drew her to Thee by the bands of love?
Not Thine? Then his?
                           Ah, Christ——the thorn-crowned Head
Bends . . . bends again . . . down on your knees, Fra
    Paolo!
If his, then Thine!
                           Kneel, priest, for this is heaven . . .

A Torchbearer

Great cities rise and have their fall; the brass
That held their glories moulders in its turn,
Hard granite rots like an uprooted weed,
And ever on the palimpsest of earth
Impatient Time rubs out the word he writ.

But one thing makes the years its pedestal,
Springs from the ashes of its pyre, and claps
A skyward wing above its epitaph—
The will of man willing immortal things.

The ages are but baubles hung upon
The thread of some strong lives—and one slight wrist
May lift a century above the dust;
For Time,
The Sisyphean load of little lives,
Becomes the globe and sceptre of the great.
But who are these that, linking hand in hand,
Transmit across the twilight waste of years
The flying brightness of a kindled hour?
Not always, nor alone, the lives that search
How they may snatch a glory out of heaven
Or add a height to Babel; oftener they
That in the still fulfilment of each day's
Pacific order hold great deeds in leash,
That in the sober sheath of tranquil tasks
Hide the attempered blade of high emprise,
And leap like lightning to the clap of fate.

So greatly gave he, nurturing 'gainst the call
Of one rare moment all the daily store
Of joy distilled from the acquitted task,
And that deliberate rashness which bespeaks
The pondered action passed into the blood;
So swift to harden purpose into deed
That, with the wind of ruin in his hair,
Soul sprang full-statured from the broken flesh,

And at one stroke he lived the whole of life,
Poured all in one libation to the truth,
A brimming flood whose drops shall overflow
On deserts of the soul long beaten down
By the brute hoof of habit, till they spring
In manifold upheaval to the sun.

Call here no high artificer to raise
His wordy monument—such lives as these
Make death a dull misnomer and its pomp
An empty vesture. Let resounding lives
Re-echo splendidly through high-piled vaults
And make the grave their spokesman—such as he
Are as the hidden streams that, underground,
Sweeten the pastures for the grazing kine,
Or as spring airs that bring through prison bars
The scent of freedom; or a light that burns
Immutably across the shaken seas,
Forevermore by nameless hands renewed,
Where else were darkness and a glutted shore.

II

The Mortal Lease

I

Because the currents of our love are poured
Through the slow welter of the primal flood
From some blind source of monster-haunted mud,
And flung together by random forces stored
Ere the vast void with rushing worlds was scored—
Because we know ourselves but the dim scud
Tossed from their heedless keels, the sea-blown bud
That wastes and scatters ere the wave has roared—

Because we have this knowledge in our veins,
Shall we deny the journey's gathered lore—
The great refusals and the long disdains,
The stubborn questing for a phantom shore,
The sleepless hopes and memorable pains,
And all mortality's immortal gains?

II

Because our kiss is as the moon to draw
The mounting waters of that red-lit sea
That circles brain with sense, and bids us be
The playthings of an elemental law,
Shall we forego the deeper touch of awe
On love's extremest pinnacle, where we,
Winging the vistas of infinity,
Gigantic on the mist our shadows saw?

Shall kinship with the dim first-moving clod
Not draw the folded pinion from the soul,
And shall we not, by spirals vision-trod,
Reach upward to some still-retreating goal,
As earth, escaping from the night's control,
Drinks at the founts of morning like a god?

III

All, all is sweet in that commingled draught
Mysterious, that life pours for lovers' thirst,
And I would meet your passion as the first
Wild woodland woman met her captor's craft,
Or as the Greek whose fearless beauty laughed
And doffed her raiment by the Attic flood;
But in the streams of my belated blood
Flow all the warring potions love has quaffed.

How can I be to you the nymph who danced
Smooth by Ilissus as the plane-tree's bole,
Or how the Nereid whose drenched lashes glanced
Like sea-flowers through the summer sea's long roll—
I that have also been the nun entranced
Who night-long held her Bridegroom in her soul?

IV

"Sad Immortality is dead," you say,
"And all her grey brood banished from the soul;
Life, like the earth, is now a rounded whole,
The orb of man's dominion. Live to-day."
And every sense in me leapt to obey,
Seeing the routed phantoms backward roll;

But from their waning throng a whisper stole,
And touched the morning splendour with decay.

"Sad Immortality is dead; and we
The funeral train that bear her to her grave.
Yet hath she left a two-faced progeny
In hearts of men, and some will always see
The skull beneath the wreath, yet always crave
In every kiss the folded kiss to be."

v

Yet for one rounded moment I will be
No more to you than what my lips may give,
And in the circle of your kisses live
As in some island of a storm-blown sea,
Where the cold surges of infinity
Upon the outward reefs unheeded grieve,
And the loud murmur of our blood shall weave
Primeval silences round you and me.

If in that moment we are all we are
We live enough. Let this for all requite.
Do I not know, some wingèd things from far
Are borne along illimitable night
To dance their lives out in a single flight
Between the moonrise and the setting star?

VI

The Moment came, with sacramental cup
Lifted—and all the vault of life grew bright
With tides of incommensurable light—

But tremblingly I turned and covered up
My face before the wonder. Down the slope
I heard her feet in irretrievable flight,
And when I looked again, my stricken sight
Saw night and rain in a dead world agrope.

Now walks her ghost beside me, whispering
With lips derisive: "Thou that wouldst forego—
What god assured thee that the cup I bring
Globes not in every drop the cosmic show,
All that the insatiate heart of man can wring
From life's long vintage?—Now thou shalt not know."

VII

Shall I not know? I, that could always catch
The sunrise in one beam along the wall,
The nests of June in April's mating call,
And ruinous autumn in the wind's first snatch
At summer's green impenetrable thatch—
That always knew far off the secret fall
Of a god's feet across the city's brawl,
The touch of silent fingers on my latch?

Not thou, vain Moment! Something more than thou
Shall write the score of what mine eyes have wept,
The touch of kisses that have missed my brow,
The murmur of wings that brushed me while I slept,
And some mute angel in the breast even now
Measures my loss by all that I have kept.

Strive we no more. Some hearts are like the bright
Tree-chequered spaces, flecked with sun and shade,
Where gathered in old days the youth and maid
To woo, and weave their dances; with the night
They cease their flutings, and the next day's light
Finds the smooth green unconscious of their tread,
And ready its velvet pliancies to spread
Under fresh feet, till these in turn take flight.

But other hearts a long long road doth span,
From some far region of old works and wars,
And the weary armies of the thoughts of man
Have trampled it, and furrowed it with scars,
And sometimes, husht, a sacred caravan
Moves over it alone, beneath the stars.

Experience

I

Like Crusoe with the bootless gold we stand
Upon the desert verge of death, and say:
"What shall avail the woes of yesterday
To buy to-morrow's wisdom, in the land
Whose currency is strange unto our hand?
In life's small market they had served to pay
Some late-found rapture, could we but delay
Till Time hath matched our means to our demand."

But otherwise Fate wills it, for, behold,
Our gathered strength of individual pain,
When Time's long alchemy hath made it gold,
Dies with us—hoarded all these years in vain,
Since those that might be heir to it the mould
Renew, and coin themselves new griefs again.

II

O Death, we come full-handed to thy gate,
Rich with strange burden of the mingled years,
Gains and renunciations, mirth and tears,
And love's oblivion, and remembering hate,
Nor know we what compulsion laid such freight
Upon our souls—and shall our hopes and fears
Buy nothing of thee, Death? Behold our wares,
And sell us the one joy for which we wait.
Had we lived longer, life had such for sale,
With the last coin of sorrow purchased cheap,
But now we stand before thy shadowy pale,
And all our longings lie within thy keep—
Death, can it be the years shall naught avail?

"Not so," Death answered, "they shall purchase sleep."

Grief

I

On immemorial altitudes august
Grief holds her high dominion. Bold the feet

That climb unblenching to that stern retreat
Whence, looking down, man knows himself but dust.
There lie the mightiest passions, earthward thrust
Beneath her regnant footstool, and there meet
Pale ghosts of buried longings that were sweet,
With many an abdicated "shall" and "must."

For there she rules omnipotent, whose will
Compels a mute acceptance of her chart;
Who holds the world, and lo! it cannot fill
Her mighty hand; who will be served apart
With uncommunicable rites, and still
Surrender of the undivided heart.

II

She holds the world within her mighty hand,
And lo! it is a toy for babes to toss,
And all its shining imagery but dross,
To those that in her awful presence stand;
As sun-confronting eagles o'er the land
That lies below, they send their gaze across
The common intervals of gain and loss,
And hope's infinitude without a strand.

But he who, on that lonely eminence,
Watches too long the whirling of the spheres
Through dim eternities, descending thence
The voices of his kind no longer hears,
And, blinded by the spectacle immense,
Journeys alone through all the after years.

Chartres

I

Immense, august, like some Titanic bloom,
   The mighty choir unfolds its lithic core,
Petalled with panes of azure, gules and or,
   Splendidly lambent in the Gothic gloom,
And stamened with keen flamelets that illume
   The pale high-altar. On the prayer-worn floor,
By worshippers innumerous thronged of yore,
   A few brown crones, familiars of the tomb,
The stranded driftwood of Faith's ebbing sea—
   For these alone the finials fret the skies,
The topmost bosses shake their blossoms free,
   While from the triple portals, with grave eyes,
Tranquil, and fixed upon eternity,
   The cloud of witnesses still testifies.

II

The crimson panes like blood-drops stigmatise
   The western floor. The aisles are mute and cold.
A rigid fetich in her robe of gold,
   The Virgin of the Pillar, with blank eyes,
Enthroned beneath her votive canopies,
   Gathers a meagre remnant to her fold.
The rest is solitude; the church, grown old,
   Stands stark and grey beneath the burning skies.
Well-nigh again its mighty framework grows
   To be a part of nature's self, withdrawn
From hot humanity's impatient woes;
   The floor is ridged like some rude mountain lawn,
And in the east one giant window shows
   The roseate coldness of an Alp at dawn.

Two Backgrounds

I

LA VIERGE AU DONATEUR

Here by the ample river's argent sweep,
Bosomed in tilth and vintage to her walls,
A tower-crowned Cybele in armoured sleep
The city lies, fat plenty in her halls,
With calm parochial spires that hold in fee
The friendly gables clustered at their base,
And, equipoised o'er tower and market-place,
The Gothic minster's winged immensity;
And in that narrow burgh, with equal mood,
Two placid hearts, to all life's good resigned,
Might, from the altar to the lych-gate, find
Long years of peace and dreamless plenitude.

II

MONA LISA

Yon strange blue city crowns a scarpèd steep
No mortal foot hath bloodlessly essayed;
Dreams and illusions beacon from its keep,
But at the gate an Angel bares his blade;
And tales are told of those who thought to gain
At dawn its ramparts; but when evening fell
Far off they saw each fading pinnacle
Lit with wild lightnings from the heaven of pain;
Yet there two souls, whom life's perversities
Had mocked with want in plenty, tears in mirth,
Might meet in dreams, ungarmented of earth,
And drain Joy's awful chalice to the lees.

The Tomb of Ilaria Giunigi

Ilaria, thou that wert so fair and dear
That death would fain disown thee, grief made wise
With prophecy thy husband's widowed eyes,
And bade him call the master's art to rear
Thy perfect image on the sculptured bier,
With dreaming lids, hands laid in peaceful guise
Beneath the breast that seems to fall and rise,
And lips that at love's call should answer "Here!"

First-born of the Renascence, when thy soul
Cast the sweet robing of the flesh aside,
Into these lovelier marble limbs it stole,
Regenerate in art's sunrise clear and wide,
As saints who, having kept faith's raiment whole,
Change it above for garments glorified.

The One Grief

One grief there is, the helpmeet of my heart,
   That shall not from me till my days be sped,
   That walks beside me in sunshine and in shade,
And hath it in all my fortunes equal part.
At first I feared it, and would often start
   Aghast to find it bending o'er my bed,
   Till usage slowly dulled the edge of dread,
And one cold night I cried: *How warm thou art!*

Since then we two have travelled hand in hand,
    And, lo, my grief has been interpreter
For me in many a fierce and alien land
Whose speech young Joy had failed to understand,
    Plucking me tribute of red gold and myrrh
From desolate whirlings of the desert sand.

The Eumenides

Think you we slept within the Delphic bower,
What time our victim sought Apollo's grace?
Nay, drawn into ourselves, in that deep place
Where good and evil meet, we bode our hour.
For not inexorable is our power,
And we are hunted of the prey we chase,
Soonest gain ground on them that flee apace,
And draw temerity from hearts that cower.

Shuddering we gather in the house of ruth,
And on the fearful turn a face of fear,
But they to whom the ways of doom are clear
Not vainly named us the Eumenides.
Our feet are faithful in the paths of truth,
And in the constant heart we house at peace.

III

Orpheus

Love will make men dare to die for their beloved . . . Of this Alcestis is a monument . . . for she was willing to lay down her life for her husband . . . and so noble did this appear to the gods that they granted her the privilege of returning to earth . . . but Orpheus, the son of Œagrus, they sent empty away . . . —PLATO: *The Symposium.*

Orpheus the Harper, coming to the gate
Where the implacable dim warder sate,
Besought for parley with a shade within,
Dearer to him than life itself had been,
Sweeter than sunlight on Illyrian sea,
Or bloom of myrtle, or murmur of laden bee,
Whom lately from his unconsenting breast
The Fates, at some capricious blind behest,
Intolerably had reft—Eurydice,
Dear to the sunlight as Illyrian sea,
Sweet as the murmur of bees, or myrtle bloom—
And uncompanioned led her to the tomb.

There, solitary by the Stygian tide,
Strayed her dear feet, the shadow of his own,
Since, 'mid the desolate millions who have died,
Each phantom walks its crowded path alone;
And there her head, that slept upon his breast,
No more had such sweet harbour for its rest,
Nor her swift ear from those disvoicèd throats
Could catch one echo of his living notes,
And, dreaming nightly of her pallid doom,
No solace had he of his own young bloom,

But yearned to pour his blood into her veins
And buy her back with unimagined pains.

To whom the Shepherd of the Shadows said:
"Yea, many thus would bargain for their dead;
But when they hear my fatal gateway clang
Life quivers in them with a last sweet pang.
They see the smoke of home above the trees,
The cordage whistles on the harbour breeze;
The beaten path that wanders to the shore
Grows dear because they shall not tread it more,
The dog that drowsing on their threshold lies
Looks at them with their childhood in his eyes,
And in the sunset's melancholy fall
They read a sunrise that shall give them all."

"Not thus am I," the Harper smiled his scorn.
"I see no path but those her feet have worn;
My roof-tree is the shadow of her hair,
And the light breaking through her long despair
The only sunrise that mine eyelids crave;
For doubly dead without me in the grave
Is she who, if my feet had gone before,
Had found life dark as death's abhorrèd shore."

The gate clanged on him, and he went his way
Amid the alien millions, mute and grey,
Swept like a cold mist down an unlit strand,
Where nameless wreckage gluts the stealthy sand,
Drift of the cockle-shells of hope and faith
Wherein they foundered on the rock of death.

So came he to the image that he sought
(Less living than her semblance in his thought),
Who, at the summons of his thrilling notes,
Drew back to life as a drowned creature floats
Back to the surface; yet no less is dead.
And cold fear smote him till she spoke and said:
"Art thou then come to lay thy lips on mine,
And pour thy life's libation out like wine?
Shall I, through thee, revisit earth again,
Traverse the shining sea, the fruitful plain,
Behold the house we dwelt in, lay my head
Upon the happy pillows of our bed,
And feel in dreams the pressure of thine arms
Kindle these pulses that no memory warms?
Nay: give me for a space upon thy breast
Death's shadowy substitute for rapture—rest;
Then join again the joyous living throng,
And give me life, but give it in thy song;
For only they that die themselves may give
Life to the dead: and I would have thee live."

Fear seized him closer than her arms; but he
Answered: "Not so—for thou shalt come with me!
I sought thee not that we should part again,
But that fresh joy should bud from the old pain;
And the gods, if grudgingly their gifts they make,
Yield all to them that without asking take."

"The gods," she said, "(so runs life's ancient lore)
Yield all man takes, but always claim their score.

The iron wings of the Eumenides
When heard far off seem but a summer breeze;
But me thou'lt have alive on earth again
Only by paying here my meed of pain.
Then lay on my cold lips the tender ghost
Of the dear kiss that used to warm them most,
Take from my frozen hands thy hands of fire,
And of my heart-strings make thee a new lyre,
That in thy music men may find my voice,
And something of me still on earth rejoice."

Shuddering he heard her, but with close-flung arm
Swept her resisting through the ghostly swarm.
"Swift, hide thee 'neath my cloak, that we may glide
Past the dim warder as the gate swings wide."
He whirled her with him, lighter than a leaf
Unwittingly whirled onward by a brief
Autumnal eddy; but when the fatal door
Suddenly yielded him to life once more,
And issuing to the all-consoling skies
He turned to seek the sunlight in her eyes,
He clutched at emptiness—she was not there;
And the dim warder answered to his prayer:
"Once only have I seen the wonder wrought.
But when Alcestis thus her master sought,
Living she sought him not, nor dreamed that fate
For any subterfuge would swing my gate.
Loving, she gave herself to livid death,
Joyous she bought his respite with her breath,
Came, not embodied, but a tenuous shade,
In whom her rapture a great radiance made.

For never saw I ghost upon this shore
Shine with such living ecstasy before,
Nor heard an exile from the light above
Hail me with smiles: *Thou art not Death but Love!*

"But when the gods, frustrated, this beheld,
How, living still, among the dead she dwelled,
Because she lived in him whose life she won,
And her blood beat in his beneath the sun,
They reasoned: 'When the bitter Stygian wave
The sweetness of love's kisses cannot lave,
When the pale flood of Lethe washes not
From mortal mind one high immortal thought,
Akin to us the earthly creature grows,
Since nature suffers only what it knows.
If she whom we to this grey desert banned
Still dreams she treads with him the sunlit land
That for his sake she left without a tear,
Set wide the gates—her being is not here.'

"So ruled the gods; but thou, that sought'st to give
Thy life for love, yet for thyself wouldst live,
They know not for their kin; but back to earth
Give, pitying, one that is of mortal birth."

Humbled the Harper heard, and turned away,
Mounting alone to the empoverished day;
Yet, as he left the Stygian shades behind,
He heard the cordage on the harbour wind,
Saw the blue smoke above the homestead trees,
And in his hidden heart was glad of these.

An Autumn Sunset

I

Leaguered in fire
The wild black promontories of the coast extend
Their savage silhouettes;
The sun in universal carnage sets,
And, halting higher,
The motionless storm-clouds mass their sullen threats,
Like an advancing mob in sword-points penned,
That, balked, yet stands at bay.
Mid-zenith hangs the fascinated day
In wind-lustrated hollows crystalline,
A wan Valkyrie whose wide pinions shine
Across the ensanguined ruins of the fray,
And in her hand swings high o'erhead,
Above the waste of war,
The silver torch-light of the evening star
Wherewith to search the faces of the dead.

II

Lagooned in gold,
Seem not those jetty promontories rather
The outposts of some ancient land forlorn,
Uncomforted of morn,
Where old oblivions gather,
The melancholy unconsoling fold
Of all things that go utterly to death
And mix no more, no more
With life's perpetually awakening breath?
Shall Time not ferry me to such a shore,

Over such sailless seas,
To walk with hope's slain importunities
In miserable marriage? Nay, shall not
All things be there forgot,
Save the sea's golden barrier and the black
Close-crouching promontories?
Dead to all shames, forgotten of all glories,
Shall I not wander there, a shadow's shade,
A spectre self-destroyed,
So purged of all remembrance and sucked back
Into the primal void,
That should we on that shore phantasmal meet
I should not know the coming of your feet?

Moonrise Over Tyringham

Now the high holocaust of hours is done,
And all the west empurpled with their death,
How swift oblivion drinks the fallen sun,
How little while the dusk remembereth!

Though some there were, proud hours that marched in
        mail,
And took the morning on auspicious crest,
Crying to fortune "Back, for I prevail!"—
Yet now they lie disfeatured with the rest;

And some that stole so soft on destiny
Methought they had surprised her to a smile;
But these fled frozen when she turned to see,
And moaned and muttered through my heart awhile.

But now the day is emptied of them all,
And night absorbs their life-blood at a draught;
And so my life lies, as the gods let fall
An empty cup from which their lips have quaffed.

Yet see—night is not . . . by translucent ways,
Up the grey void of autumn afternoon
Steals a mild crescent, charioted in haze,
And all the air is merciful as June.

The lake is a forgotten streak of day
That trembles through the hemlocks' darkling bars,
And still, my heart, still some divine delay
Upon the threshold holds the earliest stars.

O pale equivocal hour, whose suppliant feet
Haunt the mute reaches of the sleeping wind,
Art thou a watcher stealing to entreat
Prayer and sepulture for thy fallen kind?

Poor plaintive waif of a predestined race,
Their ruin gapes for thee. Why linger here?
Go hence in silence. Veil thine orphaned face,
Lest I should look on it and call it dear.

For if I love thee thou wilt sooner die;
Some sudden ruin will plunge upon thy head,
Midnight will fall from the revengeful sky
And hurl thee down among thy shuddering dead.

Avert thine eyes. Lapse softly from my sight,
Call not my name, nor heed if thine I crave,
So shalt thou sink through mitigated night
And bathe thee in the all-effacing wave.

But upward still thy perilous footsteps fare
Along a high-hung heaven drenched in light,
Dilating on a tide of crystal air
That floods the dark hills to their utmost height.

Strange hour, is this thy waning face that leans
Out of mid-heaven and makes my soul its glass?
What victory is imaged there? What means
Thy tarrying smile? Oh, veil thy lips and pass.

Nay . . . pause and let me name thee! For I see,
O with what flooding ecstasy of light,
Strange hour that wilt not loose thy hold on me,
Thou 'rt not day's latest, but the first of night!

And after thee the gold-foot stars come thick,
From hand to hand they toss the flying fire,
Till all the zenith with their dance is quick
About the wheeling music of the Lyre.

Dread hour that lead'st the immemorial round,
With lifted torch revealing one by one
The thronging splendours that the day held bound,
And how each blue abyss enshrines its sun—

Be thou the image of a thought that fares
Forth from itself, and flings its ray ahead,
Leaping the barriers of ephemeral cares,
To where our lives are but the ages' tread,

And let this year be, not the last of youth,
But first—like thee!—of some new train of hours,
If more remote from hope, yet nearer truth,
And kin to the unpetitionable powers.

All Souls

I

A thin moon faints in the sky o'erhead,
And dumb in the churchyard lie the dead.
Walk we not, Sweet, by garden ways,
Where the late rose hangs and the phlox delays,
But forth of the gate and down the road,
Past the church and the yews, to their dim abode.
For it's turn of the year and All Souls' night,
When the dead can hear and the dead have sight.

II

Fear not that sound like wind in the trees:
It is only their call that comes on the breeze;
Fear not the shudder that seems to pass:
It is only the tread of their feet on the grass;
Fear not the drip of the bough as you stoop:
It is only the touch of their hands that grope—
For the year's on the turn and it's All Souls' night,
When the dead can yearn and the dead can smite.

III

And where should a man bring his sweet to woo
But here, where such hundreds were lovers too?
Where lie the dead lips that thirst to kiss,
The empty hands that their fellows miss,
Where the maid and her lover, from sere to green,
Sleep bed by bed, with the worm between?
For it's turn of the year and All Souls' night,
When the dead can hear and the dead have sight.

IV

And now they rise and walk in the cold,
Let us warm their blood and give youth to the old.
Let them see us and hear us, and say: "Ah, thus
In the prime of the year it went with us!"
Till their lips drawn close, and so long unkist,
Forget they are mist that mingles with mist!
For the year's on the turn, and it's All Souls' night,
When the dead can burn and the dead can smite.

V

Till they say, as they hear us—poor dead, poor dead!—
"Just an hour of this, and our age-long bed—
Just a thrill of the old remembered pains
To kindle a flame in our frozen veins,
A touch, and a sight, and a floating apart,
As the chill of dawn strikes each phantom heart—
For it's turn of the year and All Souls' night,
When the dead can hear and the dead have sight."

VI

And where should the living feel alive
But here in this wan white humming hive,
As the moon wastes down, and the dawn turns cold,
And one by one they creep back to the fold?
And where should a man hold his mate and say:
"One more, one more, ere we go their way"?
For the year's on the turn, and it's All Souls' night,
When the living can learn by the churchyard light.

VII

And how should we break faith who have seen
Those dead lips plight with the mist between,
And how forget, who have seen how soon
They lie thus chambered and cold to the moon?
How scorn, how hate, how strive, we too,
Who must do so soon as those others do?
For it's All Souls' night, and break of the day,
And behold, with the light the dead are away . . .

All Saints

All so grave and shining see they come
*   From the blissful ranks of the forgiven,*
Though so distant wheels the nearest crystal dome,
*   And the spheres are seven.*

Are you in such haste to come to earth,
    Shining ones, the Wonder on your brow,
To the low poor places of your birth,
    And the day that must be darkness now?

Does the heart still crave the spot it yearned on
    In the grey and mortal years,
The pure flame the smoky hearth it burned on,
    The clear eye its tears?

Was there, in the narrow range of living,
    After all the wider scope?
In the old old rapture of forgiving,
    In the long long flight of hope?

Come you, from free sweep across the spaces,
    To the irksome bounds of mortal law,
From the all-embracing Vision, to some face's
    Look that never saw?

Never we, imprisoned here, had sought you,
    Lured you with the ancient bait of pain,
Down the silver current of the light-years brought you
    To the beaten round again—

Is it you, perchance, who ache to strain us
	Dumbly to the dim transfigured breast,
Or with tragic gesture would detain us
	From the age-long search for rest?

Is the labour then more glorious than the laurel,
	The learning than the conquered thought?
Is the meed of men the righteous quarrel,
	Not the justice wrought?

Long ago we guessed it, faithful ghosts,
	Proudly chose the present for our scene,
And sent out indomitable hosts
	Day by day to widen our demesne.

Sit you by our hearth-stone, lone immortals,
	Share again the bitter wine of life!
Well we know, beyond the peaceful portals
	There is nothing better than our strife,

Nought more thrilling than the cry that calls us,
	Spent and stumbling, to the conflict vain,
After each disaster that befalls us
	Nerves us for a sterner strain,

And, when flood or foeman shakes the sleeper
	In his moment's lapse from pain,
Bids us fold our tents, and flee our kin, and deeper
	Drive into the wilderness again.

The Old Pole Star

Before the clepsydra had bound the days
Man tethered Change to his fixed star, and said:
"The elder races, that long since are dead,
Marched by that light; it swerves not from its base
Though all the worlds about it wax and fade."

When Egypt saw it, fast in reeling spheres,
Her Pyramids shaft-centred on its ray
She reared and said: "Long as this star holds sway
In uninvaded ether, shall the years
Revere my monuments—" and went her way.

The Pyramids abide; but through the shaft
That held the polar pivot, eye to eye,
Look now—blank nothingness! As though Change
    laughed
At man's presumption and his puny craft,
The star has slipped its leash and roams the sky.

Yet could the immemorial piles be swung
A skyey hair's-breadth from their rooted base,
Back to the central anchorage of space,
Ah, then again, as when the race was young,
Should they behold the beacon of the race!

Of old, men said: "The Truth is there: we rear
Our faith full-centred on it. It was known
Thus of the elders who foreran us here,
Mapped out its circuit in the shifting sphere,
And found it, 'mid mutation, fixed alone."

Change laughs again, again the sky is cold,
And down that fissure now no star-beam glides.
Yet they whose sweep of vision grows not old
Still at the central point of space behold
Another pole-star: for the Truth abides.

A Grave

Though life should come
With all its marshalled honours, trump and drum,
To proffer you the captaincy of some
Resounding exploit, that shall fill
Man's pulses with commemorative thrill,
And be a banner to far battle days
For truths unrisen upon untrod ways,
What would your answer be,
O heart once brave?
Seek otherwhere; for me,
I watch beside a grave.

Though to some shining festival of thought
The sages call you from steep citadel
Of bastioned argument, whose rampart gained
Yields the pure vision passionately sought,
In dreams known well,
But never yet in wakefulness attained,
How should you answer to their summons, save:
I watch beside a grave?

Though Beauty, from her fane within the soul
Of fire-tongued seers descending,
Or from the dream-lit temples of the past
With feet immortal wending,
Illuminate grief's antre swart and vast
With half-veiled face that promises the whole
To him who holds her fast,
What answer could you give?
Sight of one face I crave,
One only while I live;
Woo elsewhere; for I watch beside a grave.

Though love of the one heart that loves you best,
A storm-tossed messenger,
Should beat its wings for shelter in your breast,
Where clung its last year's nest,
The nest you built together and made fast
Lest envious winds should stir,
And winged each delicate thought to minister
With sweetness far-amassed
To the young dreams within—
What answer could it win?
The nest was whelmed in sorrow's rising wave,
Nor could I reach one drowning dream to save;
I watch beside a grave.

Non Dolet!

Age after age the fruit of knowledge falls
To ashes on men's lips;
Love fails, faith sickens, like a dying tree
Life sheds its dreams that no new spring recalls;
The longed-for ships
Come empty home or founder on the deep,
And eyes first lose their tears and then their sleep.

So weary a world it lies, forlorn of day,
And yet not wholly dark,
Since evermore some soul that missed the mark
Calls back to those agrope
In the mad maze of hope,
"Courage, my brothers—I have found the way!"

The day is lost? What then?
What though the straggling rear-guard of the fight
Be whelmed in fear and night,
And the flying scouts proclaim
That death has gripped the van—
Ever the heart of man
Cheers on the hearts of men!

"*It hurts not!*" dying cried the Roman wife;
And one by one
The leaders in the strife
Fall on the blade of failure and exclaim:
"The day is won!"

A Hunting-Song

Hunters, where does Hope nest?
Not in the half-oped breast,
Nor the young rose,
Nor April sunrise—those
With a quick wing she brushes,
The wide world through,
Greets with the throat of thrushes,
Fades from as fast as dew.

But, would you spy her sleeping,
Cradled warm,
Look in the breast of weeping,
The tree stript by storm;
But, would you bind her fast,
Yours at last,
Bed-mate and lover,
Gain the last headland bare
That the cold tides cover,
There may you capture her, there,
Where the sea gives to the ground
Only the drift of the drowned.

Yet, if she slips you, once found,
Push to her uttermost lair
In the low house of despair.
There will she watch by your head,
Sing to you till you be dead,
Then, with your child in her breast,
In another heart build a new nest.

Survival

When you and I, like all things kind or cruel,
The garnered days and light evasive hours,
Are gone again to be a part of flowers
And tears and tides, in life's divine renewal,

If some grey eve to certain eyes should wear
A deeper radiance than mere light can give,
Some silent page abruptly flush and live,
May it not be that you and I are there?

Uses

Ah, from the niggard tree of Time
    How quickly fall the hours!
It needs no touch of wind or rime
    To loose such facile flowers.

Drift of the dead year's harvesting,
    They clog to-morrow's way,
Yet serve to shelter growths of spring
    Beneath their warm decay,

Or, blent by pious hands with rare
    Sweet savours of content,
Surprise the soul's December air
    With June's forgotten scent.

A Meeting

On a sheer peak of joy we meet;
   Below us hums the abyss;
Death either way allures our feet
   If we take one step amiss.

One moment let us drink the blue
   Transcendent air together—
Then down where the same old work's to do
   In the same dull daily weather.

We may not wait . . . yet look below!
   How part? On this keen ridge
But one may pass. They call you—go!
   My life shall be your bridge.

Nightingales in Provence

(i)

Whence come they, small and brown,
Miraculous and frail,
Like spring's invisible pollen blown
On the wild southern gale?
From whatsoever depth of gold and blue,
Far-templed sand and ringèd palms they wing,
Falling like dew
Upon the land, they bring
Music and spring,
With all things homely-sweet
Exhaled beneath the feet
On stony mountain-trail,
Or where green slopes, through tamarisk and pine,
Seaward decline—
Thyme and the lavender,
Where honey-bees make stir,
And the green dragon-flies with silver whirr
Loot the last rosemaries—
The morning-glory, rosy as her name,
The poppies' leaping flame
Along the kindled vines,
Down barren banks the vetches spilt like lees,
In watery meadows the great celandines

Afloat like elfin moons,
In the pale world of dunes
A foam of asphodel
Upon the sea's blue swell,
And, where the great rocks valley-ward are rolled,
The tasselled ilex-bloom fringing dark woods with gold.

Shyly the first begin—
And the thrilled ear delays,
Through a fresh veil of interblossomed mays
Straining to win
That soft sequestered note,
Where the new throat,
In some deep cleft of quietness remote,
Its budding bliss essays.
Shyly the first begin—
But, as the numerous rose
First to the hedgerow throws
A blossom here and there,
As if in hope to win
The unheeding glances of the passer-by,
And, never catching his dulled eye,
Thinks: "But my tryst is with the Spring!"
And suddenly the dusty roadside glows
With scented glory, crimsoned to its close—
So wing by wing,
Unheeded and unheard,
Bird after bird,
They come;
And where the woods were dumb,
Dumb all the streamsides and unlistening vales,

Now glory streams along the evening gales,
And all the midday is a murmuring,
Now they are come.

    (ii)
I lie among the thyme;
The sea is at my feet,
And all the air is sweet
With the capricious chime
Of interwoven notes
From those invisible and varying throats,
As though the blossomed trees,
The laden breeze,
The springs within their caves,
And even the sleeping waves,
Had all begun to sing.

Sweet, sweet, oh heavy-sweet
As tropic bales undone
At a Queen's ebon feet
In equatorial sun,
Those myriad balmy voices
Drip iterated song.
And every tiny tawny throat rejoices
To mix its separate rapture with the throng.
For now the world is theirs,
And the captivated airs
Carry no other note.
As from midsummer's throat,
Strong-pillared, organ-built,
Pours their torrential glory,

On their own waves they float,
And toss from crest to crest their cockle-shell of story—
And, as plumed breakers tilt
Against the plangent beaches,
And all the long reticulated reaches
Hiss with their silver lances,
And heave with their deep rustle of retreat
At fall of day—
So swells, and so withdraws that tidal lay
As spring advances. . . .

(iii)

I lie among the thyme,
The sea is at my feet,
And the slow-kindling moon begins to climb
To her bejewelled seat—
And now, and now again,
Mixed with her silver rain,
Listen, a rarer strain,
A tenderer fall—
And all the night is white and musical,
The forests hold their breath, the sky lies still
On every listening hill,
And far far out those straining sails,
Even as they dip and turn,
One moment backward yearn
To the rich laughter of the nightingales.

Mistral in the Maquis

Roofed in with creaking pines we lie
And see the waters burn and whiten,
The wild seas race the racing sky,
The tossing landscape gloom and lighten.

With emerald streak and silver blotch
The white wind paints the purple sea.
Warm in our hollow dune we watch
The honey-orchis nurse the bee.

Gold to the keel the startled boats
Beat in on palpitating sail,
While overhead with many throats
The choral forest hymns the gale.

'Neath forest-boughs the templed air
Hangs hushed as when the Host is lifted,
While, flanks astrain and rigging bare,
The last boat to the port has drifted. . . .

Nought left but the lost wind that grieves
On darkening seas and furling sails,
And the long light that Beauty leaves
Upon her fallen veils. . . .

Les Salettes

Let all my waning senses reach
To clasp again that secret beach,
Pine-roofed and rock-embrasured, turned
To where the winter sunset burned
Beyond a purpling dolphin-cape
On charmèd seas asleep . . .
Let every murmur, every shape,
Fanned by that breathing hour's delight,
Against the widening western deep
Hold back the hour, hold back the night. . . .

For here, across the molten sea,
From golden islands lapped in gold,
Come all the shapes that used to be
Part of the sunset once to me,
And every breaker's emerald arch
Bears closer their ethereal march,
And flings its rose and lilac spray
To dress their brows with scattered day,
As trooping shoreward, one by one,
Swift in the pathway of the sun,
With lifted arms and eyes that greet,
The lost years hasten to my feet.

All is not pain, their eyes declare;
The shoreward ripples are their voice,
The sunset, streaming through their hair,
Coils round me in a fiery flood,
And all the sounds of that rich air

Are in the beating of my blood,
Crying: *Rejoice, rejoice, rejoice!*

Rejoice, because such skies are blue,
Each dawn, above a world so fair,
Because such glories still renew
To transient eyes the morning's hue,
Such buds on every fruit-tree smile,
Such perfumes blow on every gale,
Such constellated hangings veil
The outer emptiness awhile;
And these frail senses that were thine,
Because so frail, and worn so fine,
Are as a Venice glass, wherethrough
Life's last drop of evening wine
Shall like a draught of morning shine.

The glories go; their footsteps fade
Into an all-including shade,
And isles and sea and clouds and coasts
Wane to an underworld of ghosts.
But as I grope with doubtful foot
By myrtle branch and lentisk root
Up the precipitous pine-dark way,
Through fringes of the perished day
Falters a star, the first alight,
And threaded on that tenuous ray
The age-long promise reappears,
And life is Beauty, fringed with tears.

Dieu d'Amour

(A Castle in Cyprus)

Beauty hath two great wings
That lift me to her height,
Though steep her secret dwelling clings
'Twixt earth and light.
Thither my startled soul she brings
In a murmur and stir of plumes,
And blue air cloven,
And in aerial rooms
Windowed on starry springs
Shows me the singing looms
Whereon her worlds are woven;

Then, in her awful breast,
Those heights descending,
Bears me, a child at rest,
At the day's ending,
Till earth, familiar as a nest,
Again receives me,
And Beauty veiled in night,
Benignly bending,
Drops from the sinking west
One feather of our flight,
And on faint sandals leaves me.

Segesta

High in the secret places of the hills
Cliff-girt it stands, in grassy solitude,
No ruin but a vision unachieved.

This temple is a house not made with hands
But born of man's incorrigible need
For permanence and beauty in the scud
And wreckage of mortality—as though
Great thoughts, communing in the noise of towns
With inward isolation and deep peace,
And dreams gold-paven for celestial feet,
Had wrought the sudden wonder; and behold,
The sky, the hills, the awful colonnade,
And, night-long woven through the fane's august
Intercolumniations, all the stars
Processionally wheeling—
                       Then it was
That, having reared their wonder, it would seem
The makers feared their God might prove less great
Than man's heart dreaming on him—and so left
The shafts unroofed, untenanted the shrine.

The Tryst

(*1914*)

I said to the woman: Whence do you come,
With your bundle in your hand?

She said: In the North I made my home,
Where slow streams fatten the fruitful loam,
And the endless wheat-fields run like foam
To the edge of the endless sand.

I said: What look have your houses there,
And the rivers that glass your sky?
Do the steeples that call your people to prayer
Lift fretted fronts to the silver air,
And the stones of your streets, are they washed and fair
When the Sunday folk go by?

My house is ill to find, she said,
For it has no roof but the sky;
The tongue is torn from the steeple-head,
The streets are foul with the slime of the dead,
And all the rivers run poison-red
With the bodies drifting by.

I said: Is there none to come at your call
In all this throng astray?
They shot my husband against a wall,
And my child (she said), too little to crawl,
Held up its hands to catch the ball
When the gun-muzzle turned its way.

I said: There are countries far from here
Where the friendly church-bells call,
And fields where the rivers run cool and clear,
And streets where the weary may walk without fear,
And a quiet bed, with a green tree near,
To sleep at the end of it all.

She answered: Your land is too remote,
And what if I chanced to roam
When the bells fly back to the steeples' throat,
And the sky with banners is all afloat,
And the streets of my city rock like a boat
With the tramp of her men come home?

I shall crouch by the door till the bolt is down,
And then go in to my dead.
Where my husband fell I will put a stone,
And mother a child instead of my own,
And stand and laugh on my bare hearth-stone
When the King rides by, she said.

Battle Sleep

(*1915*)

Somewhere, O sun, some corner there must be
Thou visitest, where down the strand
Quietly, still, the waves go out to sea
From the green fringes of a pastoral land.

Deep in the orchard-bloom the roof-trees stand,
The brown sheep graze along the bay.
And through the apple-boughs above the sand
The bees' hum sounds no fainter than the spray.
There through uncounted hours declines the day
To the low arch of twilight's close,
And, just as night about the moon grows gray,
One sail leans westward to the fading rose.

Giver of dreams, O thou with scatheless wing
Forever moving through the fiery hail,
To flame-seared lids the cooling vision bring
And let some soul go seaward with that sail.

Elegy

Ah, how I pity the young dead who gave
All that they were, and might become, that we
With tired eyes should watch this perfect sea
Reweave its patterning of silver wave
Round scented cliffs of arbutus and bay.

No more shall any rose along the way,
The myrtled way that wanders to the shore,
Nor jonquil-twinkling meadow any more,
Nor the warm lavender that takes the spray,
Smell only of the sea-salt and the sun,

But, through recurring seasons, every one
Shall speak to us with lips the darkness closes,
Shall look at us with eyes that missed the roses,
Clutch us with hands whose work was just begun,
Laid idle now beneath the earth we tread—

And always we shall walk with the young dead—
Ah, how I pity the young dead, whose eyes
Strain through the sod to see these perfect skies,
Who feel the new wheat springing in their stead,
And the lark singing for them overhead!

With the Tide

Somewhere I read, in an old book whose name
Is gone from me, I read that when the days
Of a man are counted and his business done,
There comes up the shore at evening, with the tide,
To the place where he sits, a boat—
And in the boat, from the place where he sits, he sees
Dim in the dusk, dim and yet so familiar,
The faces of his friends long dead; and knows
They come for him, brought in upon the tide,
To take him where men go at set of day.
Then, rising, with his hands in theirs, he goes
Between them his last steps, that are the first
Of the new life; and with the tide they pass,
Their shaken sail grown small upon the moon.

Often I thought of this, and pictured me
How many a man that lives with throngs about him,
Yet straining in the twilight for that boat
Shall scarce make out one figure in the stern,
And that so faint, its features shall perplex him
With doubtful memories—and his heart hang back.

But others, rising as they see the sail
Increase upon the sunset, hasten down,
Hands out and eyes elated; for they see,
Head over head, crowding from bow to stern,
Repeopling their long loneliness with smiles,
The faces of their friends—and such go out
Content upon the ebb-tide, with safe hearts.

But never
To worker summoned when his day was done
Did mounting tide bear such a freight of friends
As stole to you up the white wintry shingle
That night while those that watched you thought you
    slept.
Softly they came, and beached the boat, and stood
In the still cove, under the icy stars,
Your last-born and the dear loves of your heart,
And with them all the friends you called by name,
And all men that have loved right more than ease,
And honour above honours; all who gave
Free-handed of their best for other men,
And thought the giving taking; they who knew
Man's natural state is effort: up and up—
All these were there, so great a company
Perchance you marvelled, wondering what great craft
Had brought that throng unnumbered to the cove
Where the boys used to beach their light canoe
After old happy picnics,

But these your friends and children, to whose hands
Committed in the silent night you rose
And took your last faint steps—
These led you down, O great American,
Down to the winter night and the white beach;
And there you saw that the huge hull that waited
Was not as are the boats of the other dead,
Frail craft for a light passage;
But first of a long line of towering ships,
Storm-worn and Ocean-weary every one,

The ships you launched, the ships you manned, the
    ships
That now, returning from their sacred quest
With the thrice-sacred burden of their dead,
Lay waiting there to take you forth with them,
Out on the flood-tide, to some farther quest.

La folle du logis

Wild wingèd thing, O brought I know not whence
To beat your life out in my life's low cage;
You strange familiar, nearer than my flesh
Yet distant as a star, that were at first
A child with me a child, yet elfin-far,
And visibly of some unearthly breed;
Mirthfullest mate of all my mortal games,
Yet shedding on them some evasive gleam
Of Latmian loneliness—O even then
Expert to lift the latch of our low door
And profit by the hours when, dusked about
By human misintelligence, we made
Our first weak fledgling flights—
Divine accomplice of those perilous-sweet
Low moth-flights of the unadventured soul
Above the world's dim garden!—now we sit
After what stretch of years, what stretch of wings,
In the same cage together—still as near
And still as strange!
                    Only I know at last

That we are fellows till the last night falls,
And that I shall not miss your comrade hands
Till they have closed my lids, and by them set
A taper that—who knows?—may yet shine through.

Sister, my comrade, I have ached for you,
Sometimes, to see you curb your pace to mine,
And bow your Maenad crest to the dull forms
Of human usage; I have loosed your hand
And whispered: "Go! Since I am tethered here";
And you have turned, and breathing for reply:
"I too am pinioned, as you too are free,"
Have caught me to such undreamed distances
As the last planets see, when they look forth
To the sentinel pacings of the outmost stars—
Nor these alone,
Comrade, my sister, were your gifts. More oft
Has your impalpable wing-brush bared for me
The heart of wonder in familiar things,
Unroofed dull rooms, and hung above my head
The cloudy glimpses of a vernal moon,
Or all the autumn heaven ripe with stars.

And you have made a secret pact with Sleep,
And when she comes not, or her feet delay,
Toiled in low meadows of gray asphodel
Under a pale sky where no shadows fall,
Then, hooded like her, to my side you steal,
And the night grows like a great rumouring sea,
And you a boat, and I your passenger,
And the tide lifts us with an indrawn breath

Out, out upon the murmurs and the scents,
Through spray of splintered star-beams, or white rage
Of desperate moon-drawn waters—on and on
To some blue sea's unalterable calm
That ever like a slow-swung mirror rocks
The balanced breasts of sea-birds. . . .

Yet other nights, my sister, you have been
The storm, and I the leaf that fled on it
Terrifically down voids that never knew
The pity of creation—till your touch
Has drawn me back to earth, as, in the dusk,
A scent of lilac from an unseen hedge
Bespeaks the hidden farm, the bedded cows,
And safety, and the sense of human kind. . . .

And I have climbed with you by secret ways
To meet the dews of morning, and have seen
The shy gods like retreating shadows fade,
Or on the thymy reaches have surprised
Old Chiron sleeping, and have waked him not . . .

Yet farther have I fared with you, and known
Love and his sacred tremors, and the rites
Of his most inward temple; and beyond
Have seen the long grey waste where lonely thoughts
Listen and wander where a city stood.

And creeping down by waterless defiles
Under an iron midnight, have I kept
My vigil in the waste till dawn began

To walk among the ruins, and I saw
A sapling rooted in a fissured plinth,
And a wren's nest in the thunder-threatening hand
Of some old god of granite. . . .

The First Year

(*All Souls' Day*)

(i)

Here in my darkness
I lie in the depths of things,
As in a black wood whereof flowers and boughs are the
    roots,
And the moist-branching tendrils and ligaments,
Woven or spiralled or spreading, the roof of my head,
Blossomless, birdless, starless, skied with black earth,
A ponderous heaven.

But they forget,
Too often forget, and too soon, who above us
Brush the dead leaves from our mounds,
Scrape the moss from our names,
And feel safe,
They forget that one day in the year our earth becomes
    ether,
And the roots binding us loosen
As Peter's chains dropped for the Angel,
In that old story they read there;
Forget—do they seek to remember?—

That one day in the year we are with them,
Rejoin them, hear them, behold them, and walk the old
    ways with them—
One!

To-morrow . . .
And already I feel
The harsh arms of ivy-coils loosening
Like a dead man's embrace,
I feel the cool worms from my hair
Rain like dew,
And the soft-muzzled moles boring deeper,
Down after the old dead that stir not,
Or just grumble: "Don't wake me," and turn
The nether side of their skulls to their head-slab . . .
While I . . . I their one-year neighbour,
Thrusting up like a willow in spring,
From my hair
Untwine the thick grass-hair carefully,
Unbind the cool roots from my lids,
Straining up, straining up with thin hands,
Scattering the earth like a cloud,
And stopping my ears from the cry,
Lower down,
Persistent, like a sick child's wail,
The cry of the girl just below me:
"Don't go, don't go . . ." the poor coward!

    (ii)
How light the air is!
I'm dizzy . . . my feet fly up . . .

And this mad confusion of things topsy-turvey,
With the friendly comprehensible roots all hidden,
In this queer world where one can't see how things
      happen,
But only what they become . . .
Was it always so queer and inexplicable?
Yes, but the fresh smell of things . . .
Are these apples in the wet grass, I wonder?
Sweet, sweet, sweet, the smell of the living!
And the far-off sky, and the stars,
And the quiet spaces between,
So that one can float and fly . . .
Why used we only to walk?

This is the gate—and the latch still unmended!
Yet how often I told him. . . . Ah, the scent of my box-
      border!
And a late clove-pink still unfrozen.
It's what they call a "mild November" . . .
I knew that, below there, by the way the roots kept
      pushing,
But I'd forgotten how tender it was on the earth . . .
So quickly the dead forget!
And the living? I think, after all, they remember,
With everything about them so unchanged,
And no leaden loam on their eyes.
Yes, surely, I know *he* remembers;
Whenever he touches the broken latch,
He thinks: "How often she asked me,
And how careless I was not to mend it!"
And smiles and sighs; then recalls

How we planted the box-border together,
Knee to knee in the wet, one November . . .
And the clove-pinks—
Here is the window.
They've put the green lamp on the table,
Where his books lie, heaped as of old—
Ah, thank God for the old disorder!
How I used to hate it, and now—
Now I could kiss the dust on the mirror, the pipe-ashes
Over everything—all the old mess
That no strange hand interferes with . . .
Bless him for that!

(iii)
Just at first
This much contents me; why should I peer
Past the stripped arms of the rose, the metallic
Rattle of clematis dry as my hair,
There where June flushes and purples the window like
        sunset? I know
So well the room's other corner: the hearth
Where autumn logs smoulder,
The hob,
The kettle, the crane, the cushion he put for my feet,
And my Chair—
O Chair, always mine!
Do I dare?
What—the room so the same, his and mine,
Not a book changed, the inkstand uncleaned,

The old pipe-burn scarring the table,
The old rent in the rug, where I tripped
And he caught me—no woman's hand here
Has mended or marred; all's the same!
Why not dare, then? Oh, but to think,
If I stole to my chair, if I sat there,
Feet folded, arms stretched on the arms,
So quiet,
And waited for night and his coming . . .
Oh, think, when he came
And sank in the other chair, facing me,
Not a line of his face would alter,
Nor his hands fall like sun on my hair,
Nor the old dog jump on me, grinning
Yet cringing, because she half-knew
I'd found out the hole in my border,
And why my tallest auratum was dead—
But his face would be there, unseeing,
His eyes look through me;
And the old dog—not pausing
At her bowl for a long choking drink,
Or to bite the burrs from her toes, and stretch
Sideward to the fire, dreaming over their tramp in the
    stubble—
Would creep to his feet
Bristling a little . . .
And I,
I should be there, in the old place,
All the old life bubbling up in me,
And to him no more felt than the sap
Struggling up unseen in the clematis—
Ah, then, then, then I were dead!

But what *was* I, then? Lips and hands only—
Since soul cannot reach him without them?
Oh, heavy grave of the flesh,
Did I never once reach to him through you?
I part the branches and look. . . .

(iv)

O my Chair . . .
But who sits in you? One like me
Aflame yet invisible!
Only I, with eyes death-anointed,
Can see her young hair, and the happy heart riding
The dancing sea of her breast!
Then she too is waiting—
And young as I was?
Was she always there?
Were her lips between all our kisses?
Did her hands know the folds of his hair?
Did she hear what I said when I loved him?
Was the room never empty? Not once?
When I leaned in that chair, which one of us two did he
      see?
Did he feel us both on his bosom?
How strange! If I spoke to her now she would hear me,
She alone . . .
Would tell me all, through her weeping,
Or rise up and curse me, perhaps—
As I might her, were she living!

But since she is dead, I will go—
Go home, and leave them together . . .
I will go back to my dungeon,
Go back, and never return;
Lest another year, in my chair,
I find one sitting,
One whom he sees, and the old dog fears not, but
    springs on . . .
I will not suffer what *she* must have suffered, but creep
To my bed in the dark,
And mind how the girl below called to me,
Called up through the mould and the grave-slabs:
"*Do not go! Do not go! Do not go!*"

Alternative Epitaphs

"——*of heart-failure.*"

(i)

Death touched me where your head had lain.
What other spot could he have found
So tender to receive a wound,
So versed in all the arts of pain?

(ii)

Love came, and gave me wind and sun,
Love went, and left me light and air.
Nor gave he anything more fair
Than what I found when he was gone.

Only a Child

They found him hanging dead, you know,
   In the cell where he had lain
Through many a day of restless woe
   And night of sleepless pain.
The heart had ceased its beating,
   The little hands were numb,
And the piteous voice entreating
   In death at last was dumb.

No doubt it was a painful fact
   For them to contemplate;
They felt the horror of the act,
   But felt it rather late.
There was none to lay the blame to—
   That, each one understands;
And the jury found—he came to
   His death by his own hands!

Poor little hands! that should have known
   No subtler arts than these—
To seek for violets newly blown
   Beneath the April breeze,
Or gaily bind unchidden
   The daisies into sheaves,

Or reach the bird's nest hidden
    Among the budding leaves.

Poor little hands! And little heart
    That ached so long alone,
With none to ease its secret smart
    And none to hear its moan;
As he lay where they had cast him
    In the dark upon the floor,
And heard the feet go past him
    Outside his prison door.

Think of him, you whose children lie
    Soft sleeping overhead;
All day he could not see the sky,
    All night he had no bed.
Four walls of brick and mortar
    To shut the child's soul in,
And starving on bread and water
    For—some little childish sin!

So in the darkness there he lay
    While the hours crawled along,
And thought of the woodlands far away
    Awake with the robin's song;
And thought of the green grass growing
    And the boys at play outside,
And the breath of heaven blowing
    O'er the country far and wide.

Perhaps he saw his mother's face
    Bend o'er him in the gloom;
But when he leaned to catch her dress
    She vanished from the room;
And though he tried to remember
    The prayer he used to say,
In a pitiful, broken stammer
    On his lips it died away.

His little hands had nought to do
    But beat against the wall,
Until at last too tired they grew—
    Poor little hands—so small!
And so he lay there voiceless,
    Alone upon the ground;
If he wept, his tears were noiseless,
    For he feared to hear their sound.

At last perhaps the silence grew
    Too deep—it dazed his head—
And his little hands had naught to do;
    And so—they found him dead!
In a Christian town it happened,
    In a home for children built,
And God knows whose soul shall answer
    For the burden of this guilt!

But He who bade the children come
    And not be turned away,
Has surely taken the homeless home,
    And we need not mourn to-day;

For our lives are all God-given,
   The poorest to him is dear,
And the Father has room in heaven
   For the children we don't want here!

The Parting Day

I.

Some busy hands have brought to light,
   And laid beneath my eye,
The dress I wore that afternoon
   You came to say good-by.

About it still there seems to cling
   Some fragrance unexpressed,
The ghostly odor of the rose
   I wore upon my breast;

And, subtler than all flower-scent,
   The sacred garment holds
The memory of that parting day
   Close hidden in its folds.

The rose is dead, and you are gone,
   But to the dress I wore
The rose's smell, the thought of you,
   Are wed forevermore.

II.

That day you came to say good-by
  (A month ago! It seems a year!)
How calm I was! I met your eye,
  And in my own you saw no tear.

You heard me laugh and talk and jest,
  And lightly grieve that you should go;
You saw the rose upon my breast,
  But not the breaking heart below.

And when you came and took my hand,
  It scarcely fluttered in your hold.
Alas, you did not understand!
  For you were blind, and I was cold.

And now you cannot see my tears,
  And now you cannot hear my cry.
A month ago? Nay, years and years
  Have aged my heart since that good-by.

Areopagus

Where suns chase suns in rhythmic dance,
  Where seeds are springing from the dust,
Where mind sways mind with spirit-glance,
  High court is held, and law is just.

No hill alone, a sovereign bar;
    Through space the fiery sparks are whirled
That draw and cling, and shape a star,—
    That burn and cool, and form a world

Whose hidden forces hear a voice
    That leads them by a perfect plan:
"Obey," it cries, "with steadfast choice,
    Law shall complete what law began.

"Refuse,—behold the broken arc,
    The sky of all its stars despoiled;
The new germ smothered in the dark,
    The snow-pure soul with sin assoiled."

The voice still saith, "While atoms weave
    Both world and soul for utmost joy,
Who sins must suffer,—no reprieve;
    The law that quickens must destroy."

Euryalus

Upward we went by fields of asphodel,
Leaving Ortygia's moat-bound walls below;
By orchards, where the wind-flowers' drifted snow
Lay lightly heaped upon the turf's light swell;
By gardens, whence upon the wayside fell
Jasmine and rose in April's overflow;
Till, winding up in Epipolæ's wide brow,
We reached at last the lonely citadel.

There, on the ruined rampart climbing high,
We sat and dreamed among the browsing sheep,
Until we heard the trumpet's startled cry
Waking a clang of arms about the keep,
And seaward saw, with rapt foreboding eye,
The sails of Athens whiten on the deep.

Happiness

This perfect love can find no words to say.
What words are left, still sacred for our use,
That have not suffered the sad world's abuse,
And figure forth a gladness dimmed and gray?
Let us be silent still, since words convey
But shadowed images, wherein we lose
The fulness of love's light; our lips refuse
The fluent commonplace of yesterday.

Then shall we hear beneath the brooding wing
Of silence what abiding voices sleep,
The primal notes of nature, that outring
Man's little noises, warble he or weep,
The song the morning stars together sing,
The sound of deep that calleth unto deep.

Botticelli's Madonna in the Louvre

What strange presentiment, O Mother, lies
On thy waste brow and sadly-folded lips,
Forefeeling the Light's terrible eclipse
On Calvary, as if love made thee wise,
And thou couldst read in those dear infant eyes
The sorrow that beneath their smiling sleeps,
And guess what bitter tears a mother weeps
When the cross darkens her unclouded skies?

Sad Lady, if some mother, passing thee,
Should feel a throb of thy foreboding pain,
And think—"My child at home clings so to me,
With the same smile . . . and yet in vain, in vain,
Since even this Jesus died on Calvary"—
Say to her then: "He also rose again."

The Sonnet

Pure form, that like some chalice of old time
    Contain'st the liquid of the poet's thought
    Within thy curving hollow, gem-enwrought
    With interwoven traceries of rhyme,
While o'er thy brim the bubbling fancies climb,
    What thing am I, that undismayed have sought
    To pour my verse with trembling hand untaught
    Into a shape so small yet so sublime?

Because perfection haunts the hearts of men,
Because thy sacred chalice gathered up
The wine of Petrarch, Shakspere, Shelley—then
Receive these tears of failure as they drop
(Sole vintage of my life), since I am fain
To pour them in a consecrated cup.

The Last Giustiniani

O wife, wife, wife! As if the sacred name
Could weary one with saying! Once again
Laying against my brow your lips' soft flame,
Join with me, Sweetest, in love's new refrain,
Since the whole music of my late-found life
Is that we call each other "husband—wife."

And yet, stand back, and let your cloth of gold
Straighten its sumptuous lines from waist to knee,
And, flowing firmly outward, fold on fold,
Invest your slim young form with majesty
As when, in those calm bridal robes arrayed,
You stood beside me, and I was afraid.

I was afraid—O sweetness, whiteness, youth,
Best gift of God, I feared you! I, indeed,
For whom all womanhood has been, forsooth,
Summed up in the sole Virgin of the Creed,
I thought that day our Lady's self stood there
And bound herself to me with vow and prayer.

Ah, yes, that day. I sat, remember well,
Half-crook'd above a missal, and laid in
The gold-leaf slowly; silence in my cell;
The picture, Satan tempting Christ to sin
Upon the mount's blue, pointed pinnacle,
The world outspread beneath as fair as hell—

When suddenly they summoned me. I stood
Abashed before the Abbot, who reclined
Full-bellied in his chair beneath the rood,
And roseate with having lately dined;
And then—I standing there abashed—he said:
"The house of Giustiniani all lie dead."

It scarcely seemed to touch me (I had led
A grated life so long) that oversea
My kinsmen in their knighthood should lie dead,
Nor that this sudden death should set me free,
Me, the last Giustiniani—well, what then?
A monk!—The Giustiniani had been men.

So when the Abbot said: "The State decrees
That you, the latest scion of the house
Which died in vain for Venice overseas,
Should be exempted from your sacred vows,
And straightway, when you leave this cloistered place,
Take wife, and add new honors to the race,"

I hardly heard him—would have crept again
To the warped missal—but he snatched a sword
And girded me, and all the heart of men

Rushed through me, as he laughed and hailed me lord,
And, with my hand upon the hilt, I cried,
 "Viva San Marco!" like my kin who died.

But, straightway, when, a new-made knight, I stood
Beneath the bridal arch, and saw you come,
A certain monkish warping of the blood
Ran up and struck the man's heart in me dumb;
I breathed an Ave to our Lady's grace,
And did not dare to look upon your face.

And when we swept the waters side by side,
With timbrelled gladness clashing on the air,
I trembled at your image in the tide,
And warded off the devil with a prayer,
Still seeming in a golden dream to move
Through fiendish labyrinths of forbidden love.

But when they left us, and we stood alone,
I, the last Giustiniani, face to face
With your unvisioned beauty, made my own
In this, the last strange bridal of our race,
And, looking up at last to meet your eyes,
Saw in their depths the star of love arise,

Ah, then the monk's garb shrivelled from my heart,
And left me man to face your womanhood.
Without a prayer to keep our lips apart
I turned about and kissed you where you stood,
And gathering all the gladness of my life
Into a new-found word, I called you "wife!"

Life

Life, like a marble block, is given to all,
A blank, inchoate mass of years and days,
Whence one with ardent chisel swift essays
Some shape of strength or symmetry to call;
One shatters it in bits to mend a wall;
One in a craftier hand the chisel lays,
And one, to wake the mirth in Lesbia's gaze,
Carves it apace in toys fantastical.

But least is he who, with enchanted eyes
Filled with high visions of fair shapes to be,
Muses which god he shall immortalize
In the proud Parian's perpetuity,
Till twilight warns him from the punctual skies
That the night cometh wherein none shall see.

Jade

The patient craftsman of the East who made
His undulant dragons of the veinèd jade,
And wound their sinuous volutes round the whole
Pellucid green redundance of the bowl,
Chiseled his subtle traceries with the same
Keen stone he wrought them in.
                              Nor praise, nor blame,
Nor gifts the years relinquish or refuse,
But only a grief commensurate with thy soul,
Shall carve it in a shape for gods to use.

Phaedra

Not that on me the Cyprian fury fell,
    Last martyr of my love-ensanguined race;
    Not that my children drop the averted face
When my name shames the silence; not that hell
Holds me where nevermore his glance shall dwell
    Nightlong between my lids, my pulses race
    Through flying pines the tempest of the chase,
Nor my heart rest with him beside the well.

Not that he hates me; not, O baffled gods—
    Not that I slew him!—yet, because your goal
Is always reached, nor your rejoicing rods
Fell ever yet upon insensate clods,
    Know, the one pang that makes your triumph whole
    Is, that he knows the baseness of my soul.

Mould and Vase

Greek Pottery of Arezzo

Here in the jealous hollow of the mould,
Faint, light-eluding, as templed in the breast
Of some rose-vaulted lotus, see the best
The artist had—the vision that unrolled
Its flying sequence till completion's hold
Caught the wild round and bade the dancers rest—
The mortal lip on the immortal pressed
One instant, ere the blindness and the cold.

And there the vase: immobile, exiled, tame,
The captives of fulfillment link their round,
Foot-heavy on the inelastic ground,
How different, yet how enviously the same!
Dishonoring the kinship that they claim,
As here the written word the inner sound.

The Bread of Angels

At that lost hour disowned of day and night,
The after-birth of midnight, when life's face
Turns to the wall and the last lamp goes out
Before the incipient irony of dawn—
In that obliterate interval of time
Between the oil's last flicker and the first
Reluctant shudder of averted day,
Threading the city's streets (like mine own ghost
Wakening the echoes of dispeopled dreams),
I smiled to see how the last light that fought
Extinction was the old familiar glare
Of supper tables under gas-lit ceilings,
The same old stale monotonous carouse
Of greed and surfeit nodding face to face
O'er the picked bones of pleasure . . .
So that the city seemed, at that waste hour,
Like some expiring planet from whose face
All nobler life had perished—love and hate,
And labor and the ecstasy of thought—
Leaving the eyeless creatures of the ooze,

Dull offspring of its first inchoate birth,
The last to cling to its exhausted breast.

And threading thus the aimless streets that strayed
Conjectural through a labyrinth of death,
Strangely I came upon two hooded nuns,
Hands in their sleeves, heads bent as if beneath
Some weight of benediction, gliding by
Punctual as shadows that perform their round
Upon the inveterate bidding of the sun.
Again and yet again their ordered course
At the same hour crossed mine: obedient shades
Cast by some high-orbed pity on the waste
Of midnight evil! and my wondering thoughts
Tracked them from the hushed convent where there kin
Lay hived in sweetness of their prayer-built cells.
What wind of fate had loosed them from the lee
Of that dear anchorage where their sisters slept?
On what emprise of heavenly piracy
Did such frail craft put forth upon this world;
In what incalculable currents caught
And swept beyond the signal-lights of home
Did their white coifs set sail against the night?

At last, upon my wonder drawn, I followed
The secret wanderers till I saw them pause
Before the dying glare of those tall panes
Where greed and surfeit nodded face to face
O'er the picked bones of pleasure . . .
And the door opened and the nuns went in.

Again I met them, followed them again.
Straight as a thought of mercy to its goal
To the same door they sped. I stood alone.
And suddenly the silent city shook
With inarticulate clamor of gagged lips,
As in Jerusalem when the veil was rent
And the dead drove the living from the streets.
And all about me stalked the shrouded dead,
Dead hopes, dead efforts, loves and sorrows dead,
With empty orbits groping for their dead
In that blind mustering of murdered faiths . . .
And the door opened and the nuns came out.

I turned and followed. Once again we came
To such a threshold, such a door received them,
They vanished, and I waited. The grim round
Ceased only when the festal panes grew dark
And the last door had shot its tardy bolt.
"Too late!" I heard one murmur; and "Too late!"
The other, in unholy antiphon.
And with dejected steps they turned away.

They turned, and still I tracked them, till they bent
Under the lee of a calm convent wall
Bounding a quiet street. I knew the street,
One of those village byways strangely trapped
In the city's meshes, where at loudest noon
The silence spreads like moss beneath the foot,
And all the tumult of the town becomes
Idle as Ocean's fury in a shell.

Silent at noon—but now, at this void hour,
When the blank sky hung over the blank streets
Clear as a mirror held above dead lips,
Came footfalls, and a thronging of dim shapes
About the convent door: a suppliant line
Of pallid figures, ghosts of happier folk,
Moving in some gray underworld of want
On which the sun of plenty never dawns.
And as the nuns approached I saw the throng,
Pale emanation of that outcast hour,
Divide like vapor when the sun breaks through
And take the glory on its tattered edge.
For so a brightness ran from face to face,
Faint as a diver's light beneath the sea,
And as a wave draws up the beach, the crowd
Drew to the nuns.

                    I waited. Then those two
Strange pilgrims of the sanctuaries of sin
Brought from beneath their large conniving cloaks
Two hidden baskets brimming with rich store
Of broken viands—pasties, jellies, meats,
Crumbs of Belshazzar's table, evil waste
Of that interminable nightly feast
Of greed and surfeit, nodding face to face
O'er the picked bones of pleasure . . .
And piteous hands were stretched to take the bread
Of this strange sacrament—this manna brought
Out of the antique wilderness of sin.

Each seized a portion, turning comforted
From this new breaking of the elements;
And while I watched the mystery of renewal
Whereby the dead bones of old sins became
The living body of the love of God,
It seemed to me that a like change transformed
The city's self . . . a little wandering air
Ruffled the ivy on the convent wall;
A bird piped doubtfully; the dawn replied;
And in that ancient gray necropolis
Somewhere a child awoke and took the breast.

Ogrin the Hermit

Vous qui nous jugez, savez-vous quel boivre nous avons bu sur la mer?

Ogrin the Hermit in old age set forth
This tale to them that sought him in the extreme
Ancient grey wood where he and silence housed:

Long years ago, when yet my sight was keen,
My hearing knew the word of wind in bough,
And all the low fore-runners of the storm,
There reached me, where I sat beneath my thatch,
A crash as of tracked quarry in the brake,
And storm-flecked, fugitive, with straining breasts
And backward eyes and hands inseparable,
Tristan and Iseult, swooning at my feet,
Sought hiding from their hunters. Here they lay.

For pity of their great extremity,
Their sin abhorring, yet not them with it,
I nourished, hid, and suffered them to build
Their branchèd hut in sight of this grey cross,
That haply, falling on their guilty sleep,
Its shadow should part them like the blade of God,
And they should shudder at each other's eyes.

So dwelt they in this solitude with me,
And daily, Tristan forth upon the chase,
The tender Iseult sought my door and heard
The words of holiness. Abashed she heard,
Like one in wisdom nurtured from a child,
Yet in whose ears an alien language dwells
Of some far country whence the traveller brings
Magical treasure, and still images
Of gods forgotten, and the scent of groves
That sleep by painted rivers. As I have seen
Oft-times returning pilgrims with the spell
Of these lost lands upon their lids, she moved
Among familiar truths, accustomed sights,
As she to them were strange, not they to her.
And often, reasoning with her, have I felt
Some ancient lore was in her, dimly drawn
From springs of life beyond the four-fold stream
That makes a silver pale to Paradise;
For she was calm as some forsaken god
Who knows not that his power is passed from him,
But sees with trancèd eyes rich pilgrim-trains
In sands the desert blows about his feet.

Abhorring first, I heard her; yet her speech
Warred not with pity, or the contrite heart,
Or hatred of things evil: rather seemed
The utterance of some world where these are not,
And the heart lives in heathen innocence
With earth's innocuous creatures. For she said:
"Love is not, as the shallow adage goes,
A witch's filter, brewed to trick the blood.
The cup we drank of on the flying deck
Was the blue vault of air, the round world's lip,
Brimmed with life's hydromel, and pressed to ours
By myriad hands of wind and sun and sea.
For these are all the cup-bearers of youth,
That bend above it at the board of life,
Solicitous accomplices: there's not
A leaf on bough, a foam-flash on the wave,
So brief and glancing but it serves them too;
No scent the pale rose spends upon the night,
Nor sky-lark's rapture trusted to the blue,
But these, from the remotest tides of air
Brought in mysterious salvage, breathe and sing
In lovers' lips and eyes; and two that drink
Thus onely of the strange commingled cup
Of mortal fortune shall into their blood
Take magic gifts. Upon each others' hearts
They shall surprise the heart-beat of the world,
And feel a sense of life in things inert;
For as love's touch upon the yielded body
Is a diviner's wand, and where it falls
A hidden treasure trembles: so their eyes,
Falling upon the world of clod and brute,

And cold hearts plotting evil, shall discern
The inextinguishable flame of life
That girdles the remotest frame of things
With influences older than the stars."

So spake Iseult; and thus her passion found
Far-flying words, like birds against the sunset
That look on lands we see not. Yet I know
It was not any argument she found,
But that she was, the colour that life took
About her, that thus reasoned in her stead,
Making her like a lifted lantern borne
Through midnight thickets, where the flitting ray
Momently from inscrutable darkness draws
A myriad-veinèd branch, and its shy nest
Quivering with startled life: so moved Iseult.
And all about her this deep solitude
Stirred with responsive motions. Oft I knelt
In night-long vigil while the lovers slept
Under their outlawed thatch, and with long prayers
Sought to disarm the indignant heavens; but lo,
Thus kneeling in the intertidal hour
'T wixt dark and dawning, have mine eyes beheld
How the old gods that hide in these hoar woods,
And were to me but shapings of the air,
And flit and murmur of the breathing trees,
Or slant of moon on pools—how these stole forth,
Grown living presences, yet not of bale,
But innocent-eyed as fawns that come to drink,
Thronging the threshold where the lovers lay,
In service of the great god housed within

Who hides in his breast, beneath his mighty plumes,
The purposes and penalties of life.
Or in yet deeper hours, when all was still,
And the hushed air bowed over them alone,
Such music of the heart as lovers hear,
When close as lips lean, lean the thoughts between—
When the cold world, no more a lonely orb
Circling the unimagined track of Time,
Is like a beating heart within their hands,
A numb bird that they warm, and feel its wings—
Such music have I heard; and through the prayers
Wherewith I sought to shackle their desires,
And bring them humbled to the feet of God,
Caught the loud quiring of the fruitful year,
The leap of springs, the throb of loosened earth,
And the sound of all the streams that seek the sea.

So fell it, that when pity moved their hearts,
And those high lovers, one unto the end,
Bowed to the sundering will, and each his way
Went through a world that could not make them twain,
Knowing that a great vision, passing by,
Had swept mine eye-lids with its fringe of fire,
I, with the wonder of it on my head,
And with the silence of it in my heart,
Forth to Tintagel went by secret ways,
A long lone journey; and from them that loose
Their spicèd bales upon the wharves, and shake
Strange silks to the sun, or covertly unbosom
Rich hoard of pearls and amber, or let drip
Through swarthy fingers links of sinuous gold,

Chose their most delicate treasures. Though I knew
No touch more silken than this knotted gown,
My hands, grown tender with the sense of her,
Discerned the airiest tissues, light to cling
As shower-loosed petals, veils like meadow-smoke,
Fur soft as snow, amber like sun congealed,
Pearls pink as may-buds in an orb of dew;
And laden with these wonders, that to her
Were natural as the vesture of a flower,
Fared home to lay my booty at her feet.

And she, consenting, nor with useless words
Proving my purpose, robed herself therein
To meet her lawful lord; but while she thus
Prisoned the wandering glory of her hair,
Dimmed her bright breast with jewels, and subdued
Her light to those dull splendours, well she knew
The lord that I adorned her thus to meet
Was not Tintagel's shadowy King, but he,
That other lord beneath whose plumy feet
The currents of the seas of life run gold
As from eternal sunrise; well she knew
That when I laid my hands upon her head,
Saying, "Fare forth forgiven," the words I spoke
Were the breathings of his pity, who beholds
How, swept on his inexorable wings
Too far beyond the planetary fires
On the last coasts of darkness, plunged too deep
In light ineffable, the heart amazed
Swoons of its glory, and dropping back to earth
Craves the dim shelter of familiar sounds,

The rain on the roof, the noise of flocks that pass,
And the slow world waking to its daily round. . . .

And thus, as one who speeds a banished queen,
I set her on my mule, and hung about
With royal ornament she went her way;
For meet it was that this great Queen should pass
Crowned and forgiven from the face of Love.

Summer Afternoon

(Bodiam Castle, Sussex)

Not all the wasteful beauty of the year
Heaped in the scale of one consummate hour
Shall this outweigh: the curve of quiet air
That held, as in the green sun-fluted light
Of sea-caves quivering in a tidal lull,
Those trancèd towers and long unruined walls,
Moat-girdled from the world's dissolving touch,
The rook-flights lessening over evening woods,
And, down the unfrequented grassy slopes,
The shadows of old oaks contemplative
Reaching behind them like the thoughts of age.
High overhead hung the long Sussex ridge,
Sun-cinctured, as a beaker's rim of gold
Curves round its green concavity; and slow
Across the upper pastures of the sky
The clouds moved white before the herding airs
That in the hollow, by the moated walls,
Stirred not one sleeping lily from its sleep.

Deeper the hush fell; more remote the earth
Fled onward with the flight of cloud and sun,
And cities strung upon the flashing reel
Of nights and days. We knew no more of these
Than the grey towers redoubling in the moat
The image of a bygone strength transformed
To beauty's endless uses; and like them
We felt the touch of that renewing power
That turns the landmarks of man's ruined toil
To high star-haunted reservoirs of peace.
And with that sense there came the deeper sense
Of moments that, between the beats of time,
May thus insphere in some transcendent air
The plentitude of being.
Far currents feed them, from those slopes of soul
That know the rise and set of other stars
White-roaring downward through remote defiles
Dim-forested with unexplorèd thought;
Yet tawny from the flow of lower streams
That drink the blood of battle, sweat of earth,
And the broached vats of cities revelling.
All these the moments hold; yet these resolved
To such clear wine of beauty as shall flush
The blood to richer living. . . . Thus we mused,
And musing thus we felt the magic touch,
And such a moment held us. As, at times,
Through the long windings of each other's eyes
We have reached some secret hallowed silent place
That a god visits at the turn of night—
In such a solitude the moment held us.
And one were thought and sense in that profound

Submersion of all being deep below
The vexèd waves of action. Clear we saw,
Through the clear nether stillness of the place,
The gliding images of words and looks
Swept from us down the gusty tides of time,
And here unfolding to completer life;
And like dull pebbles from a sunless shore
Plunged into crystal waters, suddenly
We took the hues of beauty, and became,
Each to the other, all that each had sought.

Thus did we feel the moment and the place
One in the heart of beauty; while far off
The rooks' last cry died on the fading air,
And the first star stood white upon the hill.

High Pasture

To C. E. N.

Ashfield, November 16, 1907

Come up—come up: in the dim vale below
The autumn mist muffles the fading trees,
But on this keen hill-pasture, though the breeze
Has stretched the thwart boughs bare to meet the snow,
Night is not, autumn is not—but the flow
Of vast, ethereal and irradiate seas,
Poured from the far world's flaming boundaries
In waxing tides of unimagined glow.

And to that height illumined of the mind
He calls us still by the familiar way,
Leaving the sodden tracks of life behind,
Befogged in failure, chilled with love's decay—
Showing us, as the night-mists upward wind,
How on the heights is day and still more day.

Belgium

La Belgique ne regrette rien.

Not with her ruined silver spires,
Not with her cities shamed and rent,
Perish the imperishable fires
That shape the homestead from the tent.

Wherever men are staunch and free,
There shall she keep her fearless state,
And, homeless, to great nations be
The home of all that makes them great.

The Hymn of the Lusitania

(*Translated from the German*)

The swift sea sucks her death shriek under
As the great ship reels and leaps asunder;
Crammed taffrail-high with her murderous freight,
Like a straw on the tide she whirls to her fate.

A war ship she, though she lacked its coat,
And lustful for lives as none afloat.
A war ship, and one of the foe's best workers,
Not penned with her rusting harbor shirkers.
Now the Flanders guns lack their daily bread,
And shipper and buyer are sick with dread;
For, neutral as Uncle Sam may be,
Your surest neutral's the deep, green sea.
Just one ship sunk with lives and shell,
And thousands of German graycoats—well!
And for each of her graycoats German hate
Would have sunk ten ships with all their freight.
Yea, ten such ships are a paltry fine
For one good life in our fighting line.
Let England ponder the crimson text—
"Torpedo, strike! And hurrah for the next!"

The Great Blue Tent

Come unto me, said the Flag,
Ye weary and sore opprest;
For I am no shot-riddled rag,
But a great blue tent of rest.

Ye heavy laden, come
On the aching feet of dread,
From ravaged town, from murdered home,
From your tortured and your dead.

All they that beat at my crimson bars
Shall enter without demur,
Though the round earth rock with the wind of wars,
Not one of my folds shall stir.

See, here is warmth and sleep,
And a table largely spread.
I give garments to them that weep,
And for gravestones I give bread.

But what, through my inmost fold,
Is this cry on the winds of war?
Are you grown so old, are you grown so cold,
O Flag that was once our star?

Where did you learn that bread is life,
And where that fire is warm—
You, that took the van of a world-wide strife,
As an eagle takes the storm?

Where did you learn that men are bred
Where hucksters bargain and gorge;
And where that down makes a softer bed
Than the snows of Valley Forge?

Come up, come up to the stormy sky,
Where our fierce folds rattle and hum,
For Lexington taught us how to fly,
And we dance to Concord's drum.

O flags of freedom, said the Flag,
Brothers of wind and sky;
I too was once a tattered rag,
And I wake and shake at your cry.

I tug and tug at the anchoring place,
Where my drowsy folds are caught;
I strain to be off on the old fierce chase
Of the foe we have always fought.

O People I made, said the Flag,
And welded from sea to sea,
I am still the shot-riddled rag,
That shrieks to be free, to be free.

Oh, cut my silken ties
From the roof of the palace of peace;
Give back my stars to the skies,
My stripes to the storm-striped seas!

Or else, if you bid me yield,
Then down with my crimson bars.
And o'er all my azure field
Sow poppies instead of stars.

"On Active Service"

AMERICAN EXPEDITIONARY FORCE

(R. S., *August 12th, 1918*)

He is dead that was alive.
How shall friendship understand?
Lavish heart and tireless hand
Bidden not to give or strive,
Eager brain and questing eye
Like a broken lens laid by.

He, with so much left to do,
Such a gallant race to run,
What concern had he with you,
Silent Keeper of things done?

Tell us not that, wise and young,
Elsewhere he lives out his plan.
Our speech was sweetest to his tongue,
And his great gift was to be man.

Long and long shall we remember,
In our breasts his grave be made.
It shall never be December
Where so warm a heart is laid,
But in our saddest selves a sweet voice sing,
Recalling him, and Spring.

You and You

(To the American private in the great war)

Every one of you won the war—
You and you and you—
Each one knowing what it was for,
And what was his job to do.

Every one of you won the war,
Obedient, unwearied, unknown,
Dung in the trenches, drift on the shore,
Dust to the world's end blown;
Every one of you, steady and true,
You and you and you—
Down in the pit or up in the blue,
Whether you crawled or sailed or flew,
Whether your closest comrade knew
Or you bore the brunt alone—

All of you, all of you, name after name,
Jones and Robinson, Smith and Brown,
You from the piping prairie town,
You from the Fundy fogs that came,
You from the city's roaring blocks,
You from the bleak New England rocks
With the shingled roof in the apple boughs,
You from the brown adobe house—
You from the Rockies, you from the Coast,
You from the burning frontier-post
And you from the Klondyke's frozen flanks,
You from the cedar-swamps, you from the pine,

You from the cotton and you from the vine,
You from the rice and the sugar-brakes,
You from the Rivers and you from the Lakes,
You from the Creeks and you from the Licks
And you from the brown bayou—
You and you and you—
You from the pulpit, you from the mine,
You from the factories, you from the banks,
Closer and closer, ranks on ranks,
Airplanes and cannon, and rifles and tanks,
Smith and Robinson, Brown and Jones,
Ruddy faces or bleaching bones,
After the turmoil and blood and pain
Swinging home to the folks again
Or sleeping alone in the fine French rain—
Every one of you won the war.

Every one of you won the war—
You and you and you—
Pressing and pouring forth, more and more,
Toiling and straining from shore to shore
To reach the flaming edge of the dark
Where man in his millions went up like a spark,
You, in your thousands and millions coming,
All the sea ploughed with you, all the air humming,
All the land loud with you,
All our hearts proud with you,
All our souls bowed with the awe of your coming!

Where's the Arch high enough,
Lads, to receive you,
Where's the eye dry enough,
Dears, to perceive you,
When at last and at last in your glory you come,
Tramping home?

Every one of you won the war,
You and you and you—
You that carry an unscathed head,
You that halt with a broken tread,
And oh, most of all, you Dead, you Dead!

Lift up the Gates for these that are last,
That are last in the great Procession.
Let the living pour in, take possession,
Flood back to the city, the ranch, the farm,
The church and the college and mill,
Back to the office, the store, the exchange,
Back to the wife with the babe on her arm,
Back to the mother that waits on the sill,
And the supper that's hot on the range.

And now, when the last of them all are by,
Be the Gates lifted up on high
To let those Others in,
Those Others, their brothers, that softly tread,
That come so thick, yet take no ground,
That are so many, yet make no sound,
Our Dead, our Dead, our Dead!

O silent and secretly-moving throng,
In your fifty thousand strong,
Coming at dusk when the wreaths have dropt,
And streets are empty, and music stopt,
Silently coming to hearts that wait
Dumb in the door and dumb at the gate,
And hear your step and fly to your call—
Every one of you won the war,
But you, you Dead, most of all!

Lyrical Epigrams

I
My little old dog:
A heart-beat
At my feet.

II *Spring*
A winter wind,
Primroses,
And the new furrow.

III *Friendship*
The silence of midnight,
A dying fire,
And the best unsaid. . . .

IV

A pointed steeple
Above square trees—
Rustic France.

V

A blunt steeple
Over round trees—
Rural England.

VI *Soluntum*

Across these giant ruins
The greatest cloud-shadows
Dart like little lizards.

Garden Valedictory

I will not say that you are dead, but only
Scattered like seed upon the autumn breeze,
 Renewing life where all seemed locked and lonely,
 Stored in shut buds and inarticulate trees,

So that this earth, this meaningless earth, may yet
 Regain some sense for me, because a word
 You spoke in passing trembles in the jet
  Of the frail fountain in my garden-close,
 Because you stopped one day before this rose,
Or I can hear you in the migrant bird
 Throating goodbye along the lime-tree aisle,
  And feel your hand in mine, and breathe awhile.

Had I Been Only

Had I been only that which you enjoyed,
Nought were I now but old grimacing bones,
Masking with painted lips rheumatic groans,
The spectre of past pleasures that have cloyed,
The blossomed shade where Amaryllis toyed
Turned to a wilderness of stumps and stones,
Or gaunt Næera, among kindred crones,
Superfluous, meddlesome and unemployed.

Best comradeship, how frail a tie it is,
Though we entreat of it its sure delights!
Can any love our days that loved our nights,
Or feign contentment who has fed on bliss?
Not lips alone become too old to kiss;
Yet, O my other soul—was I but this?

Treasure

When unregarding Death shall come,
Pick me up and take me home—
The long long way—
Compose my eye-lids, hush the noise,
And put away the broken toys
At close of day;

If underneath my cleansèd lid
One secret vision may be hid,
Let it be
A purple shallow over-leant
By emerald pines the wind has bent,
And, when the evening sky grows pale,
A single umber-coloured sail
At sea.

Intense Love's Utterance

To—— To Whom?

As we sit, you and I, in the twilight
And breathe the soft breath of the roses
That mingled with lily and iris
Steals up from your quaint garden-closes;
In the mystical, soft evening weather
When the sunset burns amber and clear
I think that a life-time together
Would not be half long enough, dear!

I long—how I long, my heart's Lady,
To call you a name that is dearer,
To be—always your slave and your lover
And in time something fonder and nearer.
Come home to me, darling, my Lady!
Let the name that I call you be wife.
The house stands there waiting and ready,
It waits for its light and its life!

So I long in the twilight to tell you—
But there, if I pause and dissemble,
Or turn with a jest to the roses,
It is that I inwardly tremble
At the vision of taking you, Sweetest,

To a home where I could not provide
High art, the highest, completest,
To welcome my utterest Bride.

How far would a poor fellow's income
Extend in your dados and friezes,
Your Chippendale table, your ceiling
From a study of Paul Veronese's,
Your old Venice glass opalescent,
Your golden stamped leather from Spain,
Your majolica ware iridescent—
Yet to live without these would be pain.

And how could I furnish your boudoir
With sweet silver tissues (cash payment)
And make your portières out of chasubles
And ecclesiastical raiment?
And how could I give you gold panels
With wailing wan women in rows,
And sunflowers worked on green flannels,
And triptychs with carved doors to close?

You are used to a Crown Denby tea-set,
And your tea pot is always Queen Anne, dear;
Could you bear to pour out from Britannia
Into plain white and gilt—if you can, dear—
But, no! for I *know* that your sideboard
Has always been classic "Empire",
And though I could always provide board
You must count out such luxuries, dear.

And the Japanese vases, and palm-leaves,
The dim-silver church-lamp and censer,
The church-stall with wormy intarsia,
All the treasures intense and intenser,
From the bit of Limoges like a jewel
To the altar-lace under the frieze—
My Love, it were cruelly cruel
To ask you to live without these!

No, no—what is life? A succession
Of fleeting pulsations (as Pater
Has told us in Renaissance Studies)
Which must cease for us sooner or later,
And Art can alone make them precious,
And lovely and dear as old plate—
Go back to your dados and friezes,
For love is a thing out of date!

Song

Mirth of life's blooming time, sweet beyond seeming,
Lilies that laugh with the dews of the morning,
Grasses that glitter with gifts of the rain,
Roses like kisses, & kisses as fragrant
As roses that cradle June's velvet-barred vagrant,
All these I had of thee when I was glad of thee,
Now thou are gone from me, what shall remain?

Blush of the sunrise & blaze of the sunset,
Stars that are born of the gloom after moonset,
Planets that swim in the sea of the dusk,
Bird-song like laughter, & laughter as thrilling
As all the dawn's rapture of jubilant trilling,
All these I had of thee when I was glad of thee,
Now the fruit's eaten, I hold but the husk.

Gifts

When we, who walk in paths unneighbourly,
Beyond the gateway of the grave shall meet,
I shall make answer, as you pause & greet,
"Of all life's gifts what gifts have you for me?
Like masks across a crowded ballroom, we
Stumbled through life with unfamiliar feet,
And passed each other as strangers in the street,
Yet all the while you held my soul in fee!—

"Behold my gifts, the sunset none but I
Remembered, or the book none other read;
The picture that I treasured for your eye;
And, last of all, these bitterest tears unshed—
Take them! but, if you bring no gift, go by,
And leave me doubly dead among the dead."

October in Newport

Grey rocks, that lean against this perfect sky
And measureless expanse of silver sea;
Slow clouds of Autumn, poising calm & high
In windless depths of blue tranquility;
    Thwart cedar-boughs, that show
How long & bitterly the storm-winds blow
When Winter lays his hand upon the lea;

Brown hollows, tapestried with purple plume
Of late-blown asters, golden-rod's light head;
And the pale mallow's evanescent bloom,
No sooner loosened to the light than shed;
    Dark alders, close beset
With scarlet beads, & roses lingering yet
Though all your Summer sisterhood has fled,

And, O thou sea, winged with a fleet of dreams,
An argosy of longings, fairer far
Than any charmèd fishing-sail that gleams
At eventide against the sunset's bar,
    When the new moon holds sway
Above the darkling spaces of the day,
And the red West shakes forth a sudden star,

Lo, to these eyes that loved you from their birth,
No dreaming isle in waters hyaline,
No happy valley of this radiant earth,
No snow-wrapt peaks that tower above the pine,
    Lords of the lonely air,
Though for a crown the very dawn they wear,
With your transfiguring light shall ever shine.

Cynthia

He found her in the street one night. She said:
"I sin to get my mother's daily bread;
I know no other way; I never learned
To cook or sew"—& deep his anger burned
That the child's shame should feed the mother's mouth,
And so, in pity of her piteous youth,
Her sixteen years made up of bitter nights,
And short days shorn of natural delights,
He took her home. Her pinched & pretty face
Wore, with the passing months, a graver grace,
A light as if of youth won back again
After long stress of peril & of pain,
Regenerate in love's sight. He taught her hands
All that a woman's household still commands,
Her puzzled eyes to read, her lips to speak
Gentlest words only, & her heart to seek
His trustfully, till she to him became
A daughter, & to hide her cast of shame
From the world's eye he called her Cynthia Grey,
Child of a friend who, dying far away
In tropic ardours, left the girl to him.
And in the minds of both the past grew dim,
She dazzled with the dawn of hope, & he
Washing her white in pity's boundless sea,
Till both forgot that each of them had been
Led to the other by the hand of sin.

Scarce of this tranquil life five years were sped
When his sole nephew came to him & said,

"I love your friend's child, Cynthia; she will be
My wife if you are willing"—whereat he,
To whom the boy was dearer than a son,
Cursed in his heart the deed that he had done,
And, venting his self-anger on the head
He loved the best, with sudden violence said:
"No more of this, for it shall never be,
Though your entreaties storm me like the sea
Storming the shore. Why, there are fairer far
Than she is, for the asking."

                       "Though there are,"
The nephew answered, "there are none for me.
Save this one woman only, & why not she?"

"Why not? Why not? The girl is scarce of age,
Lacks gold, & has no hope of heritage"—

"But I have both," the lover answered; "find
Some better way than that to turn my mind
From loving Cynthia."

                    Then the Uncle said,
"Now for your mother's sake, my sister dead,
Ask me no more. While I have breath of life,
I swear you shall not take the girl to wife!"

"God be my witness that I shall," the lad
Replied half-smiling, & the look he had
Maddened the other, thinking that his race
Should bear the imprint of a harlot's face
In after years, & his dead sister's child
Rear children from a life-spring so defiled

With currents of vile blood without a name,
Fed from a shameless ancestry of shame,
And from his lips the sudden answer broke,
"Since on your head the lightning you invoke,
Listen—I found your Cynthia in the street,
Mixed with the mire that clung about my feet,
And in vain pity, snatched her from the slough,
Washing the mud from her smirched lips & brow;
But what she was, deeper than what she is,
Lives on, red-branded with corruption's kiss."

But still the lover, though his lips had paled,
Stood resolute. "Perchance you had prevailed
Had I not loved her, but Love can still make whole
The broken body & the blasted soul."

"What? Will you shelter with your mother's name
The forehead blazoned with the brand of shame?
What? Will you touch with consecrated love
The lips a hundred lips grew weary of
Ere yours caressed them? Shall your children's eyes
Taunt you with half-suspected prophecies
Of evil, & the patter of their feet
Remind you hers have wandered in the street?"

"Love is a god, & Love can make," he said,
"New heavens & Earth, & Love can raise the dead
Face of lost innocence from charnel-caves
Of death & darkness; Love is a pool whose waves
Bring healing to the leprous limbs of sin,
And pure as snow are they that wash therein."

And then the other, for a little space,
Was silent, till the lad's uplifted face
Of visionary triumph stung his pride,
And "take her then to be your wife," he cried,
"(If even at this your love makes no demur)
Who was my mistress ere I rescued her!"

With lifted hand, as if to fend a blow
Too heavy to be borne, & head bent low,
The lover heard him, all the refluent blood
Back-ebbing to his heart—when there she stood,
Cynthia, her hand upon the door, her face
Paler than his, & for a moment's space
All three were speechless; then the girl began—

"Is there no mercy in the heart of man
That he should joy to trample in the dust
Those whom his brothers' hands have downward thrust?
Yet kinder those that bind us in the mire,
Than these who lead our groping footsteps higher,
Then fling us down—I never asked to be
Dressed in this robe of new-born purity
You mocked me with. God knows, until you came,
Though I went naked, that I felt no shame,
But you have taught me how to blush, & you
Have taught me how to hide my guilt from view,
And wear the mask of virtue, till I dreamed
That I had grown as holy as I seemed,
And now you teach me that the Christ, who died
To wash the world of sin, was crucified
For men, but not for women"—

                                  then the door
Closed on her, & pale & speechless as before
The two men faced each other, till at last
Forth from his Uncle's face the nephew passed.

That evening Cynthia vanished. He who stood
Alone among the ruins of the good
That he had wrought from evil saw, aghast,
His empty life that fluttered in grief's blast
Like a forsaken nest. She came no more,
Nor did he seek her, though his heart was sore
And many a night he dreamed that she had come.
She came no more—but, to his desolate home
As he returned one night with laggard feet,
Shuddering he heard her laughter in the street.

"O Love, let the world for once go by"

O Love, let the world for once go by,
With its danger-signals & warning cry,
Or else let us dream it was swung in space
Just that we two might stand face to face,
Soul within soul, as eye within eye,
Deaf, blind to all else save the you & the me—
Ah, for once, my life, let the whole world be!
What! We had promised? The words were not ours—
What! There's a heart dead? But ours are just born—

Ay, what will it matter, when all are dead,
That we died apart, with one word unsaid?

"When I am gone, recall my hair"

When I am gone, recall my hair,
Not for the light it used to hold,
But that your touch, enmeshèd there,
Has turned it to a younger gold.

Recall my hands, that were not soft
Or white or fine beyond expressing,
Till they had slept so long and oft,
So warm and close, in your possessing.

Recall my eyes, that used to lie
Blind pools with summer's wreckage strewn.
You cleared the drift, but in their sky
You hung no image but your own.

Recall my mouth, that knew not how
A kiss is cradled and takes wing,
Yet fluttered like a nest-hung bough
When you had touched it like the Spring.

Senlis

Hung high against the perfect blue,
Like flame the belfry trembled higher,
Like leafage let the bird-flights through,
Like incense wreathed its melting spire.

From the dim vantage, lilac-hung,
Niched in the Roman rampart's strength,
We watched the foaming clouds that swung
Against the church's island-length,

The sheet of emerald foliage spread
Like some deep inlet's inmost reach,
Between the cliff-like towers o'erhead,
The low slate roofs that formed their beach—

We watched, & felt the tides of time
Coil round our hidden leafy place,
Sweep on through changing race & clime,
And leave us at the heart of space,

In some divine transcendent hush
Where light & darkness melt & cease,
Staying the awful cosmic rush
To give two hearts an hour of peace . . .

So deep the peace, so ours the hour,
When night-fall & the fiery train
Had swept us from our high-built bower,
And out across the dreaming plain,

Stillness yet brooded in our souls,
And even our rushing chariot stayed,
Loitering through aisles of silvery boles
In some remote & star-laced glade,

Where, through the pale & secret night,
Past gleams of water, depths of shade,
Under a low moon's golden light
We felt the quiet fields outspread—

And there, in the dim air afloat,
While silence held the throbbing train,
Some thrush, from immemorial throat,
Poured all the sweetness, all the pain.

The Coming of the God

I

As when, far off upon the sun-pale skies
Of a clear region of enormous heat,
The golden train from some dim desert seat
Of fabled empire grows upon the eyes,
A fleck, a cloud, a sea of Orient dyes,
And, high beneath his blinding canopies,
The God invisible—so beat by beat
My body hears the coming of the feet
Innumerable of surging ecstasies.

And as the city garlands every street
Before her wild & dithyrambic throng
I tremble into flower & flame to meet
The fury of the cymbal & the song—
Till suddenly the flood of rapture falls
And silence darkens down the temple walls . . .

II

Strange as some Mystery that paints the vast
Cloud-building arches of a shadowy fane
With Life's vertiginous & tragic train,
Wild as the star-sown melodies amassed
In ancient forests where great gales have passed
And shaken all their secrets loose again,
Divine as Life, and dear as Death and, last,
Endless as thou, O labyrinthine Pain,

Are the long windings of the mystic way
Up to that orient and unshadowed height
Where sense & spirit, wingèd and grown one,
Captives of loveliness, a moment stay,
Before they loose the fringes of the sun
And plunge into his blind abyss of light.

III

What power is this that gathers in its hold
All beauty & all terror, all things near
And known as childhood, fanciful as Fear,
Ghostly as sea-gleams over foundered gold,
And lovelier than the face of gods grown old,
Drawn to one murmur in the sense's ear,
As though the prisoned vastness of the sphere
Lay like a dew-drop in a rose's fold?

Lie still & let me look into your eyes,
If haply I may read where we have been,
What sights beyond all seeing we have seen,
And from what verge of unimagined awe
Brought back the spoils of what divine emprise.
Ah, close your eyes. They see not what I saw . . .

Terminus

Wonderful was the long secret night you gave me, my
     Lover,
Palm to palm, breast to breast in the gloom. The faint
     red lamp,
Flushing with magical shadows the common-place room
     of the inn,
With its dull impersonal furniture, kindled a mystic
     flame
In the heart of the swinging mirror, the glass that has
     seen
Faces innumerous & vague of the endless travelling
     automata,
Whirled down the ways of the world like dust-eddies
     swept through a street,
Faces indifferent or weary, frowns of impatience or pain,
Smiles (if such there were ever) like your smile and mine
     when they met
Here, in this self-same glass, while you helped me to
     loosen my dress,
And the shadow-mouths melted to one, like sea-birds
     that meet in a wave—
Such smiles, yes, such smiles the mirror perhaps has
     reflected;
And the low wide bed, as rutted and worn as a
     high-road,
The bed with its soot-sodden chintz, the grime of its
     brasses,
That has borne the weight of fagged bodies, dust-
     stained, averted in sleep,

The hurried, the restless, the aimless—perchance it has
    also thrilled
With the pressure of bodies ecstatic, bodies like ours,
Seeking each other's souls in the depths of unfathomed
    caresses,
And through the long windings of passion emerging
    again to the stars . . .
Yes, all this through the room, the passive & featureless
    room,
Must have flowed with the rise & fall of the human
    unceasing current;
And lying there hushed in your arms, as the waves of
    rapture receded,
And far down the margin of being we heard the low
    beat of the soul,
I was glad as I thought of those others, the nameless, the
    many,
Who perhaps thus had lain and loved for an hour on the
    brink of the world,
Secret and fast in the heart of the whirlwind of travel,
The shaking and shrieking of trains, the night-long
    shudder of traffic,
Thus, like us they have lain & felt, breast to breast in
    the dark,
The fiery rain of possession descend on their limbs
    while outside
The black rain of midnight pelted the roof of the
    station;
And thus some woman like me, waking alone before
    dawn,
While her lover slept, as I woke & heard the calm stir of
    your breathing,

Some woman has heard as I heard the farewell shriek of
the trains
Crying good-bye to the city & staggering out into
darkness,
And shaken at heart has thought: "So must we forth in
the darkness,
Sped down the fixed rail of habit by the hand of
implacable fate—
So shall we issue to life, & the rain, & the dull dark
dawning;
You to the wide flare of cities, with windy garlands and
shouting,
Carrying to populous places the freight of holiday
throngs;
I, by waste lands, & stretches of low-skied marsh
To a harbourless wind-bitten shore, where a dull town
moulders & shrinks,
And its roofs fall in, & the sluggish feet of the hours
Are printed in grass in its streets; & between the
featureless houses
Languid the town-folk glide to stare at the entering
train,
The train from which no one descends; till one pale
evening of winter,
When it halts on the edge of the town, see, the houses
have turned into grave-stones,
The streets are the grassy paths between the low roofs
of the dead;
And as the train glides in ghosts stand by the doors of
the carriages;

And scarcely the difference is felt—yea, such is the life I
  return to . . ."
Thus may another have thought; thus, as I turned may
  have turned
To the sleeping lips at her side, to drink, as I drank
  there, oblivion. . . .

"She said to me: 'Nay, take my body and eat'"

She said to me: "Nay, take my body and eat,
And give it beauty, breaking it for bread.
Or else, your hunger sated, drain instead
The chalice of my soul, wherein, to meet
Your longed-for lips, the bitter and the sweet
Of passion's mystic vintage have been shed,
And through the clear cold crystals of the head
Tremble the ardours of the central heat."

She said: "Your thirst appeasèd, rest you yet
A quiet moment in the thought of me . . .
Then pass upon your way, and quite forget;
Or dimly—as one inland feels the sea—
Recall that once a summer hour long set
Hung over you the murmur of leaf and bee . . ."

Ex Tenebrae

The Black Harp

I play for your delight
On a Harp with seven black strings.
My harp is a sleepless night,
And here are the songs it sings.

I. *"Jures-moi . . ."*

Choose not to swear your faith
    By some shared ecstasy,
But by the body of this death—
    The change in you and me.

Love's easy, when each kiss
    Lets the warm Psyche out,
But bitter when the mouth of bliss
    Wears the fixed grin of doubt.

If you would ease my heart
    Swear by some day of pain,
When our sullen footsteps dragged apart
    Just the length of habit's chain,

When you saw me proud and hard,
    And I knew you weak of will,
The god in each debased and marred—
    And we loved each other still.

II. Daphne

Youth, seize the nymph while morning's on your brow,
And in her eyes illimitable air,
When every willow is her shaken hair,
And her hand tapers from each laurel bough.

Hold her while noon is in your kiss; but when
The light of fantasy begins to set,
Weep not, O man, her waning face, but let
The nymph become the laurel once again.

III. White Death

I dreamed I lay upon the bitter ground,
A winter midnight black above my head—
The cold was on me like a pall of lead,
The white snow fell and fell without a sound,
In barbèd flakes that probed me to the bone.
Even on my burning mouth they did not melt,
But falling, falling, turned it into stone.
I woke.
          It was your kisses I had felt.

Restoration

You said: "She is not young enough—and yet
She might have been worth having. What if Love,
With those strange drugs he makes of dead men's hopes,
Should trick her to a semblance of flushed youth,

Just while a kiss endures?"

>Love, summoned, came,

And wrought with his old pigments, pain & fear;
Painted her lids with weeping, dusked her eyes
With gloom of sleepless midnights, shed the grey
Powder of ashen dawns upon her head,
And dimpled her thin cheeks with sobs indrawn.
Then, his work done, he set it in the light,
And laughed, and called to you.

>You came & looked.

"What dream deluded me? Good God, she's old!"
"Ah, that's my *patina*!" Love grinned, but you:
"The thing is ruined. I refuse to pay."

The Room

Flesh of my flesh, you walls
That saw him when he came,
How your curtained silence calls
His name, his name, his name!

You pillows of my bed,
Where he stooped, where he laid his head,
Window where, as we lay,
The summer night turned grey,
And the singing stars looked in,
Saw us, & knew their kin—

You threshold, where he turned,
And went not while he went,
Door, whence his first look yearned,
Door, whence his last was sent—

O, all my world in the world,
Heart in my breast, O room!
That held a million spheres unfurled—
And are straiter now than a tomb . . .

Rambouillet

The dark accumulated shade lies deep
As all the dead year's leaves, beneath the new
Recurrent verdure: such a shade as seems
To still the tread, & weight the wings of speech
With velvet silences, so that our words
O'er hidden thoughts flit low & languidly,
Like pale crepuscular moths that gleam & droop
Over an unseen garden. Here we sit,
As prisoned in some block of lambent jade,
Through which the light waves dim as through the sea,
While all the outer world, in spires of heat,
Winds white about us, tapering to a flame.

"You come between me & the night"

You come between me & the night.
Closer than sleep you lie with me.
You are the air, you are the light,
You are my hearing, you my sight,
And you are all I hear & see . . .

Beaumetz, February 23rd. 1915

(*Jean du Breuil de St. Germain*)

So much of life was sudden thrust
Under this dumb disfiguring dust,
Such laughter, hopes, impatient power,
Such visions of a rounded hour,
Such ardour for things deep and great,
Such easy disregard of fate,
Such memories of strange lands remote,
Of solitudes where eagles float,
Of plains where under other stars
Strange races lock in alien wars,
And isles of spicery that sleep
Unroused on an unfurrowed deep—

All this—and then his voice, his eyes,
His eager questions, gay replies,
The warmth he put into the air—
And, oh, his step upon the stair!

Poor grave, too narrow to contain
Such store of life, in vain, in vain,
The grass-roots and the ivy-ropes
Shall pinion all those springing hopes,
In vain the ivy and the grass
Efface the sense of what he was,
Poor grave!—for he shall burst your ties,
And come to us with shining eyes,
And laughter, and a quiet jest,
Whenever we, who loved him best,
Speak of great actions simply done,
And lives not vain beneath the sun.

BIOGRAPHICAL NOTE

Edith Wharton—born Edith Newbold Jones on January 24, 1862, in New York City—was the third and last child and only daughter of George Frederic Jones and Lucretia Stevens Rhinelander, both from socially prominent New York families. As a child, she lived with her family in England, Italy, France, and Germany; returning to the United States in 1872, they divided their time between Manhattan and Newport, Rhode Island. In 1878, with her mother's help, she published *Verses*, a private edition of her poetry. She married Edward Wharton in 1885, and they spent several months every year in Europe. She began to publish poems and short stories in *Scribner's*, *Harper's*, and *Century Magazine*. In 1891, she purchased a townhouse in New York, and in 1893 an estate in Newport; with architect Ogden Codman she wrote *The Decoration of Houses* (1897), which sold unexpectedly well. Her first collection of short stories, *The Great Inclination*, was published in 1899, followed by *Critical Instances* (1901), and a historical novel, *The Valley of Decision* (1902). In 1902 she moved into The Mount, a house in Lenox, Massachusetts, she helped to design. She bought an automobile in 1904, touring Sussex with close friend Henry James, and motoring across France. She continued to publish fiction—*The*

House of Mirth (1905), *Madame de Treymes* (1907), *The Fruit of the Tree* (1907), *Ethan Frome* (1911), *The Reef* (1912), and *The Custom of the Country* (1913)—and collected her poems in *Artemis to Actæon* (1909) and *Twelve Poems* (1926). In 1908 she began an affair with journalist William Morton Fullerton. The following year, her husband admitted to embezzling money from her trust funds, and she was granted a divorce in 1913 on grounds of adultery. In 1914, she visited North Africa and Spain. She devoted herself to charitable work during World War I, establishing American Hostels for Refugees and organizing the Children of Flanders Rescue Committee; she was named Chevalier of the Legion of Honor in 1916. In 1918, she bought a house in St. Brice-sous-Forêt, outside Paris. Her later fiction included *Summer* (1917), *The Marne* (1918), *The Age of Innocence* (1920), *The Old Maid* (1921), *The Glimpses of the Moon* (1922), *A Son at the Front* (1923), *The Mother's Recompense* (1925), *The Children* (1928), *Hudson River Bracketed* (1929), and *The Gods Arrive* (1932). In 1923 she became the first woman to receive an honorary doctorate of letters from Yale. An autobiography, *A Backward Glance*, was published in 1934. In July 1937 she suffered a stroke, and died at St. Brice on August 11, 1937.

NOTE ON THE TEXTS

This volume includes the complete texts of Edith Wharton's three published books of poetry—*Verses* (Newport: C. E. Hammett Jr., 1878), *Artemis to Actæon, and Other Verse* (New York: Scribner's, 1909), and *Twelve Poems* (London: Medici Society, 1926)—along with most of the poems she arranged to publish during her lifetime but did not include in one of her collections and a selection of the many poems she left in manuscript form.

The texts of Wharton's three books have been taken from the first printings. Of the three, only *Artemis to Actæon* was reprinted during her lifetime—in a British edition (London: Macmillan, 1909), prepared from the American proof sheets. Some of the poems in her books had previously appeared in periodicals, sometimes in different form.

Texts of the uncollected poems are arranged in chronological order of first known publication. They have been taken from the following sources:

Only a Child: *New York World* (May 30, 1879): 5. (Signed "Eadgyth")

The Parting Day: *Atlantic Monthly* 45 (February 1880): 194.

Areopagus: *Atlantic Monthly* 45 (March 1880): 194.

Euryalus: *Atlantic Monthly* 64 (December 1889): 761.

Happiness: *Scribner's* 6 (December 1889): 715.

Botticelli's Madonna in the Louvre: *Scribner's* 9 (January 1891): 74.

The Sonnet: *Century* 43 (November 1891): 113.

The Last Giustiniani: *Scribner's* 15 (June 1894): 405–06.

Life: *Scribner's* 15 (June 1894): 739.

Jade: *Century* 49 (January 1895): 391.

Phaedra: *Scribner's* 23 (January 1898): 68.

Mould and Vase: *Atlantic Monthly* 88 (September 1901): 343.

The Bread of Angels: *Harper's* 105 (September 1902): 583–85.

Ogrin the Hermit: *Atlantic Monthly* 104 (December 1909): 844–88.

Summer Afternoon: *Scribner's* 49 (March 1911): 277–78.

High Pasture: *Letters of Charles Eliot Norton*, vol. 2 (Boston: Houghton Mifflin, 1913): 387.

Belgium: *King Albert's Book* (London: Hodder and Stoughton, 1915): 165.

The Hymn of the Lusitania (translated from the German): *New York Herald* (Paris edition), May 7, 1915.

The Great Blue Tent: *New York Times* August 25, 1915.

"On Active Service": *Scribner's* 64 (November 1918): 619.

You and You: *Scribner's* 65 (February 1919): 152.

Lyrical Epigrams: *Yale Review* 9 (January 1920): 348.

Garden Valedictory: *Scribner's* 83 (January 1928): 81.

Had I Been Only: *Scribner's* 84 (August 1928): 215.

Treasure: *Muse Anthology of Modern Poetry*, Dorothy Kissling and Arthur H. Nethercot, eds. (New York: Carlyle Straub, 1938): 614.

The texts of Wharton's manuscript poems have been taken from a variety of manuscript and published sources, listed below; 12 are published here for the first time. An attempt has been made to arrange the manuscript poems in chronological order of composition, but in most cases—indicated by square brackets—dates assigned to the poems are conjectural. For untitled poems, titles have been supplied by enclosing the first line in quotation marks.

Beinecke   Edith Wharton Collection. Yale Collection of American Literature. Beinecke Rare Book and Manuscript Library.

Lilly   The Lilly Library, Indiana University, Blooming-
           ton, Indiana. Reprinted by permission.

Ransom   Harry Ransom Humanities Research Center. The
           University of Texas at Austin. Reprinted by per-
           mission.

Intense Love's Utterance: ms. Beinecke. *September 13, 1881.*

Song ("Mirth of life's blooming time"): ms. Lilly. *[c. 1891–93].*

Gifts: ms. Lilly. *[c. 1891–93].*

October in Newport: ms. Lilly. *[c. 1891–93].*

Cynthia: ms. Lilly. *[c. 1891–93].*

"O Love, let the world for once go by": ms. Lilly. *[c. 1891–93].*

"When I am gone, recall my hair": R.W.B. Lewis, *Edith
     Wharton: A Biography* (New York: Harper and Row, 1975):
     227. *[May 1908].*

Senlis: ms. Ransom. *May 17 [1908?].* Inscribed "For M.F."

The Coming of the God: ms. Beinecke. *[1909?]* (A copy in
     the handwriting of Morton Fullerton, at Simmons Col-
     lege, is titled "Colophon to *The Mortal Lease*").

Terminus: ms. Beinecke, in the hand of Morton Fullerton.
     June 1909. First published, in slightly different form, in
     R.W.B. Lewis, *Edith Wharton: A Biography* (New York:
     Harper and Row, 1975): 259–60.

"She said to me: 'Nay, take my body and eat'": Clare
     Colquitt, "Unpacking Her Treasures: Edith Wharton's
     'Mysterious Correspondence' with Morton Fullerton,"
     The Library Chronicle of the University of Texas at Austin,
     new series 31 (1985): 87. *April 14 [1910].*

Ex Tenebrae. ms. Beinecke. *[c. 1910?]*

Restoration: ms. Beinecke. *[c. 1910?]*

The Room: ms. Beinecke. *[c. 1910?]*

Rambouillet: ms. Beinecke. *[c. 1910?]*

"You come between me & the night": Adeline R. Tintner,
     "An Unpublished Love Poem of Edith Wharton," *Ameri-
     can Literature* 60.1 (March 1988): 98. *[1911?]*

Beaumetz, February 23rd. 1915: ts. with Wharton's auto-
     graph corrections, Lilly. *February 23, 1915.* First published

in Julie Olin-Ammentorp, *Edith Wharton's Writings from the Great War* (Gainesville: University Press of Florida, 2004): 235–36.

The texts of the original printings, typescripts, and manuscripts chosen for inclusion here are presented without change, except for the correction of typographical errors. Spelling, punctuation, and capitalization are often expressive features and are not altered, even where inconsistent or irregular. The copy of Wharton's *Verses* used in preparing this edition, from the Morgan Library, includes five handwritten emendations of apparent typographical errors (by page and line number: 6.8, chamberings; 6.20, dearest and; 17.22, sorrow; 20.19, Fill; 23.12, still once); these emendations have been adopted in the present volume.

The editor and The Library of America wish to thank Clare Colquitt and the late Scott Marshall, whose research efforts on an unpublished collection of Wharton's poetry have been of great assistance in the preparation of the present volume.

NOTES

2.12   *Bettine to Goethe*]   Bettina von Arnim (1785–1855) published an
epistolary account of her friendship with Goethe, *Goethes Briefwechsel mit
einem Kinde*, in 1835; her English translation of the book appeared in
1837 as *Goethe's Correspondence with a Child*.

3.2   *"O primavera! Gioventù dell'anno."*]   From the opening of Act III of
Il pastor fido (1590) by Giovanni Battista Guarini (1538–1612), a section
of the play often set to music, notably by Claudio Monteverdi
(1567–1643).

9.13   Gif]   *Archaic*: if.

9.14   braw]   Splendid, attractive, pretty.

35.22   Vesalius in Zante]   Wharton's note: "Vesalius, the great
anatomist, studied at Louvain and Paris, and was called by Venice to the
chair of surgery in the University of Padua. He was one of the first phys-
iologists to dissect the human body, and his great work 'The Structure of
the Human Body' was an open attack on the physiology of Galen. The
book excited such violent opposition, not only in the Church but in the
University, that in a fit of discouragement he burned his remaining man-
uscripts and accepted the post of physician at the Court of Charles V.,
and afterward of his son, Philip II. of Spain. This closed his life of free
enquiry, for the Inquisition forbade all scientific research, and the dissec-
tion of corpses was prohibited in Spain. Vesalius led for many years the
life of the rich and successful court physician, but regrets for his past
were never wholly extinguished, and in 1561 they were roused afresh by
the reading of an anatomical treatise by Gabriel Fallopius, his successor
in the chair at Padua. From that moment life in Spain became intolerable
to Vesalius, and in 1563 he set out for the East. Tradition reports that this

journey was a penance to which the Church condemned him for having opened the body of a woman before she was actually dead; but more probably Vesalius, sick of his long servitude, made the pilgrimage a pretext to escape from Spain.

"Fallopius had meanwhile died, and the Venetian Senate is said to have offered Vesalius his old chair; but on the way home from Jerusalem he was seized with illness, and died at Zante in 1564."

60.3   LA VIERGE AU DONATEUR]   Jan Van Eyck's *La Vierge au Chancelier Rolin* (1435), in the Louvre.

61.1   Tomb of Ilaria Giunigi]   Jacopo della Quercia's marble tomb of Ilaria del Carretto (1379–1405), wife of Paolo Giunigi, is in the Cathedral of San Martino at Lucca, Italy.

108.2   Only a Child]   When it was first published, this poem was prefaced by the following editorial note: "The *Press* of May 27 publishes an account of the suicide in the House of Refuge at Philadelphia of a boy who was only twelve years old. He was locked up in solitary confinement. They found him hanging by the neck dead and cold. Tired of waiting for the release that never came, he had at last escaped—from that House of Refuge!"

125.13   *Vous qui nous jugez . . . la mer?*]   From *Le Roman de Tristan et Iseult* (1900) by Joseph Bédier. In Hilaire Belloc's 1903 translation, the sentence reads: "You that sit in judgment upon us here, do you know what cup it was we drank upon the high sea?"

133.16   C. E. N.]   Charles Eliot Norton (1827–1908), Harvard professor of the history of art.

160.1   Terminus]   The manuscript of this poem, in the hand of Morton Fullerton, is followed by a note: "Poem written by E. W. during my month in America, and commemorating, in the inspiration of Goethe's *Roman Elegies*, the night which we spent at Charing Cross Hotel, before I sailed from Southampton. We had motored from Paris to Boulogne, & crossed to Folkestone when we passed the night. On the morrow we went up to London, and were met at dinner by Henry James. I took an appartment (two chambers & salon) no. 92, in which I left her alone the next day at 10, with only time to have sent to her room a bunch of roses. That evening at sea I received the accompanying telegram. M.F. Aug. 1909."

INDEX OF TITLES

ABOUT THIS SERIES

The American Poets Project offers, for the first time in our history, a compact national library of American poetry. Selected and introduced by distinguished poets and scholars, elegant in design and textually authoritative, the series makes widely available the full scope of our poetic heritage.

For other titles in the American Poets Project, or for information on subscribing to the series, please visit: www.americanpoetsproject.org.

ABOUT THE PUBLISHER

The Library of America, a nonprofit publisher, is dedicated to preserving America's best and most significant writing in handsome, enduring volumes, featuring authoritative texts. For a free catalog, to subscribe to the series, or to learn how you can help support The Library's mission, please visit www.loa.org or write: The Library of America, 14 East 60th Street, New York, NY 10022.

AMERICAN POETS PROJECT

1. **EDNA ST. VINCENT MILLAY** / J. D. McClatchy, editor

2. **POETS OF WORLD WAR II** / Harvey Shapiro, editor

3. **KARL SHAPIRO** / John Updike, editor

4. **WALT WHITMAN** / Harold Bloom, editor

5. **EDGAR ALLAN POE** / Richard Wilbur, editor

6. **YVOR WINTERS** / Thom Gunn, editor

7. **AMERICAN WITS** / John Hollander, editor

8. **KENNETH FEARING** / Robert Polito, editor

9. **MURIEL RUKEYSER** / Adrienne Rich, editor

10. **JOHN GREENLEAF WHITTIER** / Brenda Wineapple, editor

11. **JOHN BERRYMAN** / Kevin Young, editor

12. **AMY LOWELL** / Honor Moore, editor

13. **WILLIAM CARLOS WILLIAMS** / Robert Pinsky, editor

14. **POETS OF THE CIVIL WAR** / J. D. McClatchy, editor

15. **THEODORE ROETHKE** / Edward Hirsch, editor

16. **EMMA LAZARUS** / John Hollander, editor

17. **SAMUEL MENASHE** / Christopher Ricks, editor

18. **EDITH WHARTON** / Louis Auchincloss, editor

19. **GWENDOLYN BROOKS** / Elizabeth Alexander, editor